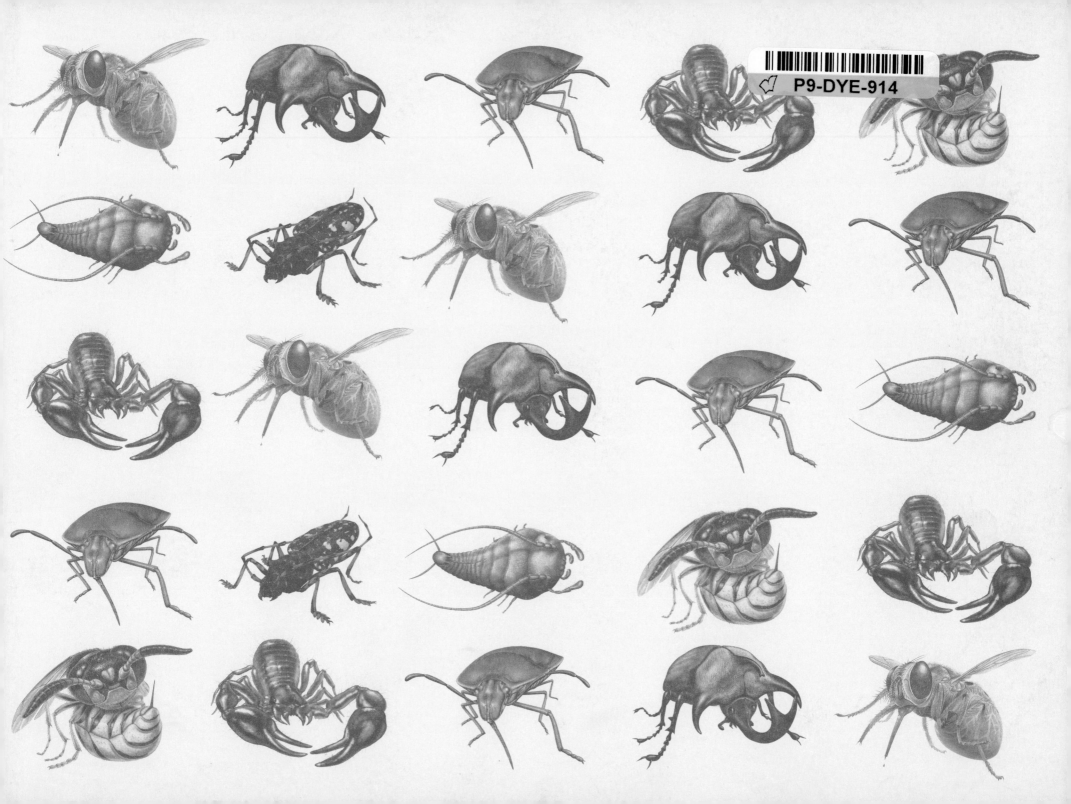

BUGS

BUGS

THE WORLD'S MOST TERRIFYING INSECTS

General Editor: Susan Barraclough

BACK**PACK**BOOKS
○
NEW YORK

Copyright © 2005 IMP AB

This 2005 edition published by Backpack Books, by arrangement with Amber Books ltd.

All rights reserved. No part of this book may be used or reproduced in any manner whatsoever without the written permission of the Publisher.

Backpack Books
122 Fifth Avenue
New York, NY 10011

ISBN 0-7607-6560-X

Printed and bound in Italy

05 06 07 08 MCH 10 9 8 7 6 5 4 3 2 1

Library of Congress Cataloging-in-Publication Data available upon request.

Editorial and design by
Amber Books Ltd
74–77 White Lion Street
London
N1 9PF
United Kingdom
www.amberbooks.co.uk

Project Editor: Tom Broder
Designer: Joe Conneally

All illustrations © IMP AB

Contents

Introduction

Bee Assassin Bug

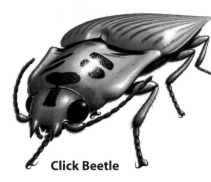

Click Beetle

Peanut Bug

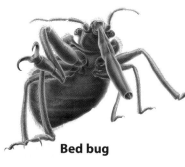

Bed bug

There are more than one million different kinds of bugs and insects on Earth, and new types are discovered every year. In fact, there are more insects on the planet than any other kind of creature. That includes human beings. There are around two million insects for every single one of us. Insects are found all over the world and live in every possible environment. Some bugs live in very cold climates, like the Arctic, although most prefer the warm, wet regions of Earth.

Bugs and creepy-crawlies come in many different shapes, sizes, and colors. All true insects have three main body parts: a head, a middle section or thorax, and an abdomen. They have antennas or feelers on their heads and use them to pick up smells or for touching. True insects also have three pairs of legs. But there are lots of other types of creepy-crawlies too, such as eight-legged spiders and mites. The little woodlouse is actually a type of land-living crustacean. In fact,

Stag Beetle

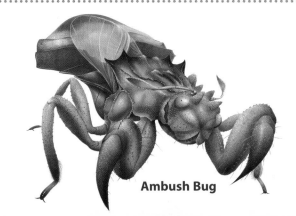

Ambush Bug

Chagas Bug

Fogstand Beetle

Stink Bug

it is more closely related to crabs and lobsters than it is to insects like beetles.

Some insects, such as butterflies or moths, are beautiful to look at. Others are not so pretty. Many bugs have some very nasty habits. Some bite. Some sting. Some spread diseases. Some, like ants, can invade your house. Others, such as locusts, can eat up an entire field of corn or wheat in a few minutes. So if they are such a nuisance, why do we need bugs and insects?

Insects have a lot of important work to do. They let air into the ground, helping farmers grow food. Bees and other insects fertilize plants and flowers so they can keep on growing year after year. Ants and beetles dig tunnels. This lets rainwater into the ground, which helps plants grow. Insects are also nature's garbagemen: They eat up trash lying on the ground. Every bug, however beastly, has its own role to play. No wonder insects always look so busy!

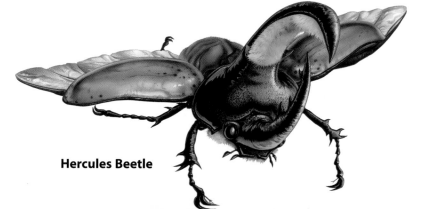

Hercules Beetle

Colorado Beetle

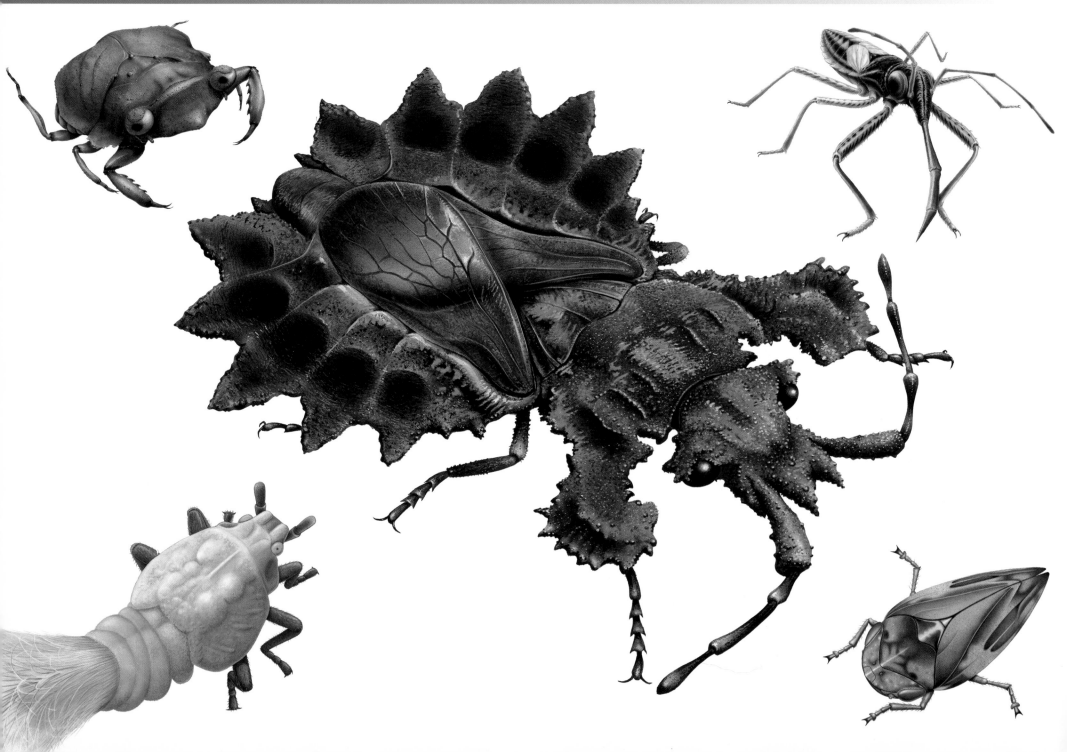

Bugs

The word "bug" is often used to describe any type of small creepy-crawly insect. But when scientists use the word, they are usually talking about a very particular type of insect.

True bugs belong to the insect family called Hemiptera. These insects have oval, flattened bodies and mouths that let them suck blood or juices from plants, animals, or humans. The aphid bug, for example, sucks sap from plants. Aphids don't look very pretty, but they are harmless. You can't say the same about bed bugs, though. Bedbugs live in our beds and suck our blood for food.

Many bugs have warlike names. One, the ambush bug, lies in wait for its victims. The bee assassin bug kills and eats other insects—"assassin" means "killer."

Spittle bugs are very destructive. They destroy crops like sugarcane, and cause serious damage to pine or willow trees. Stink bugs gives off a foul smell when they are disturbed.

It's not just other insects and plants that need to be wary of these little creatures. Some types of blood-sucking bugs, called Chagas bugs, can cause a very unpleasant disease. The huge toe-biter bug got its name by creeping up on humans dangling their feet into water and grabbing hold of their toes. Bugs like these aren't very nice to know.

APHID
Latin name: Family Aphididae

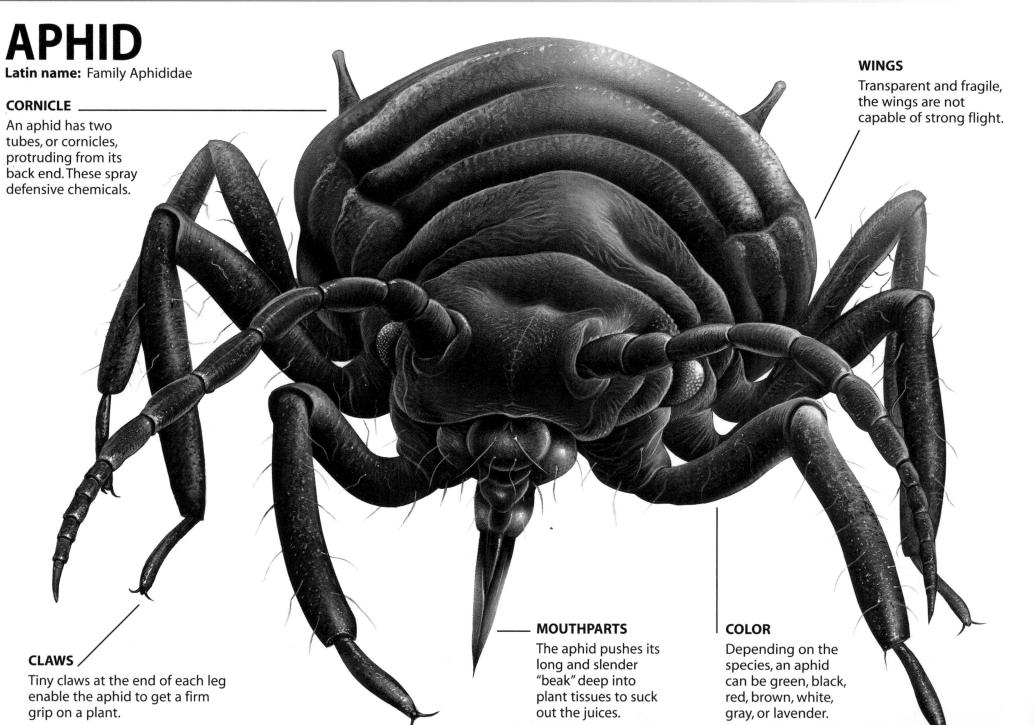

CORNICLE
An aphid has two tubes, or cornicles, protruding from its back end. These spray defensive chemicals.

WINGS
Transparent and fragile, the wings are not capable of strong flight.

CLAWS
Tiny claws at the end of each leg enable the aphid to get a firm grip on a plant.

MOUTHPARTS
The aphid pushes its long and slender "beak" deep into plant tissues to suck out the juices.

COLOR
Depending on the species, an aphid can be green, black, red, brown, white, gray, or lavender.

S quash it, spray poison on it, and even wage biological war against it, the aphid always returns in vast numbers. The secret of the pest's success is that it is an amazing breeding machine. The aphid is able to reproduce very rapidly, with or without a mate.

While it sucks up sap from a plant, an aphid can produce several daughters in quick succession. Within hours of their birth, these are also producing young. In a matter of days, a single aphid can give rise to an infestation.

HOW BIG IS IT?

x10

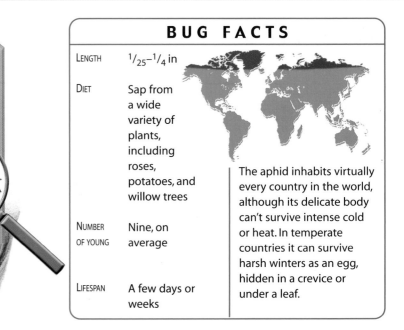

BUG FACTS

LENGTH	$1/25$–$1/4$ in
DIET	Sap from a wide variety of plants, including roses, potatoes, and willow trees
NUMBER OF YOUNG	Nine, on average
LIFESPAN	A few days or weeks

The aphid inhabits virtually every country in the world, although its delicate body can't survive intense cold or heat. In temperate countries it can survive harsh winters as an egg, hidden in a crevice or under a leaf.

On the summer host plant, an unmated aphid gives birth to exact copies of herself, called clones (1). A winged female from this brood flies to the winter host plant (2) and gives birth to her own clones (3). As the fall approaches, a male appears and mates with a female. The female lays eggs (4), which she glues to the plant stem to last out the winter. In the spring, the eggs hatch into nymphs (5). Each female produces more clones (6). This brood includes a winged female (7) that flies to the summer host plant to start the cycle over again.

Did You Know?

● If bad weather and predators didn't kill vast numbers of aphids each year, infestation would be so great that it would be impossible to grow food crops in some areas.

● Some species of ant carry aphid eggs into their nests to protect them from the cold of winter, then carry the newly hatched aphid nymphs out to food plants in the spring.

● There are over 3,800 species of aphid worldwide—and probably hundreds more yet to be discovered. Aphids are also called plant lice. Certain species are better known as greenfly (such as *Cryptomyzus ribes*) and blackfly (such as *Aphis fabae*).

● Anti-aphid measures range from industrial pesticides to baby powder and diluted dishwashing liquid.

● The green peach aphid, which attacks an enormous number of common flowers, can transmit up to 100 plant viruses as it feeds.

BEE ASSASSIN BUG

Latin name: *Apiomerus* species

EYES
Compound eyes help the bug spot prey approaching from any direction.

ANTENNAS
Sensitive antennas help the bee assassin bug find insect prey.

HAIRS
Hairs sensitive to vibration and movement cover the bee assassin bug's legs.

FRONT LEGS
The first pair of legs are thick and powerful. The bee assassin bug uses them to hold its struggling victims.

LEGS
The bee assassin bug can straddle a victim with its long legs.

BODY
The bee assassin has a stout, oval body, in direct contrast to its tiny head.

BEAK
The beak is sharp and hollow like a doctor's syringe. It folds away underneath the bee assassin's body when not in use.

FEET
The bee assassin bug has tiny claws on its feet to help it grip as it climbs around.

These powerful predators lurk on flower heads, ready to feed greedily on other insects as they fly in to sip nectar. A bee's venomous sting makes it a dangerous adversary, but it is no match for the aggressive bee assassin bug.

Seized in long, strong legs and impaled by the bug's sharp beak, the bee has little chance to put up a fight before deadly toxins flood its body. Once the bee's insides are turned to juice, a pump in the bug's narrow head soon drains the body dry.

1 Crouched on a flower, a bee assassin bug makes no attempt to hide. But a hungry bee buzzes in to feed despite the danger. It is probably attracted by the bug's special scent.

HOW BIG IS IT?

Actual Size

BUG FACTS

LENGTH	1–1 1/5 in	
PREY	Often bees, but also other nectar-feeding insects	Bee assassin bugs of the *Apiomerus* genus are natives of the Americas. They are found in many of the southwestern states of the USA, through Mexico and Central America to the northern countries of South America—wherever there are flowers and bees.
WEAPONS	Syringelike rostrum armed with fast-acting venom and digestive enzymes	
LIFESPAN	Unknown	

2 As the bee lands, the bug seizes its prey with its strong front legs. It stabs its victim with its beak and injects a mix of paralyzing venom and saliva.

3 Moments later, the bee's insides begin to dissolve. The bug sucks up the slush like drinking a milk shake through a straw.

Did You Know?

 ● When the bee assassin stabs its prey, it aims for a point near the head so the nerve toxins in its venom pass rapidly into the victim's brain.

● A bee assassin's venom contains a potent mix of toxins, and if it bites a human, the effects can be more painful than a bee or wasp sting.

● Enzymes in the bee assassin's saliva destroy the bonds that hold complex protein molecules together.

● Although the bee assassin's beak is strong and sharp, it also has delicate sensory hairs near the tip that enable the bug to feel its prey.

● When a bee assassin bug is alarmed, it makes a chirping sound like a grasshopper by scraping tiny teeth on the tip of its snout against a ridged groove beneath its body.

● Some bee assassin bugs can spit their saliva up to 35 inches, squirting it out at a rate of 16 spits per second.

FUNGUS BUG

Latin name: Family Aradidae

MOUTHPARTS

Hidden in a protective sac inside the head is a set of long, coiled mouthparts called stylets. The bug unfurls these mouthparts to their full length when it is feeding.

WINGS

The fungus bug has a pair of wings, but it rarely flies.

ANTENNAS

The short antennas are perfect for life in narrow spaces. Each one is covered in touch and scent receptors to help the bug locate fungi.

LEGS

Short legs are typical of insects that scurry around narrow spaces.

EXOSKELETON

The covering, or exoskeleton, has a rough texture. It is covered with ridges, pits, and short spines.

nder the surface of many a moldy tree stump lives a strange-looking beast. It is a bug with mouthparts many times as long as its body, and a taste for fungal growths.

The fungus bug's wrinkled, flattened body is disguised to look like a lump of tree bark. Its threadlike feeding tube uncoils from its head like a hose. When not in use, the long mouth stylets are rolled up and stored in a sac at the front of the bug's head.

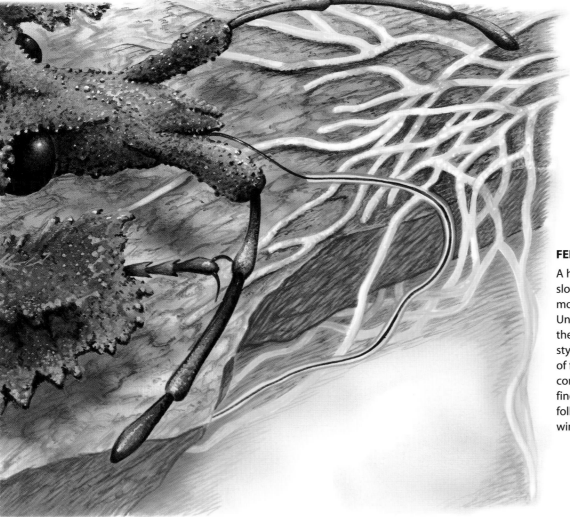

HOW BIG IS IT?

Actual Size

BUG FACTS

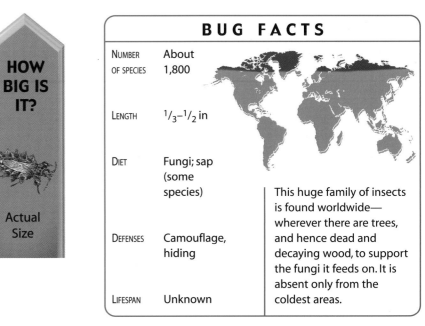

NUMBER OF SPECIES	About 1,800
LENGTH	$1/3$–$1/2$ in
DIET	Fungi; sap (some species)
DEFENSES	Camouflage, hiding
LIFESPAN	Unknown

This huge family of insects is found worldwide—wherever there are trees, and hence dead and decaying wood, to support the fungi it feeds on. It is absent only from the coldest areas.

FEEDING ON FUNGUS

A hungry fungus bug slowly extends its delicate mouthparts, or stylets. Unwinding as it probes, the insect pushes the stylets into a single strand of fungus to lap up the contents. The stylets are so fine and flexible they can follow the fungus as it winds deep into the wood.

Did You Know?

● The male of some species of fungus bug attracts females with a mating call, made by rubbing his legs against pegs or grooves on his abdomen. This is called stridulating.

● When mating, a pair of fungus bugs adopt an unusual position. The male lies below the female and clasps her with special gripping appendages on his abdomen.

● Fungus bugs are unusual among insects in that both females and males have been known to guard their offspring against predators.

● Spectacular massed flights of fungus bugs have been recorded in the USA, when huge numbers of the insects take to the wing in company with wood-boring beetles, heading for new sources of food.

● Fungus bugs often form mass feeding groups. Over 100 adults and nymphs of *Aradus betulae* have been counted living on a single fungus.

TOE-BITER
Latin name: Family Belostomatidae

WINGS
The wings, which are crossed over on the toe-biter's back, seal a bubble of air. This allows the bug to breathe underwater.

EYES
Huge compound eyes give the toe-biter good underwater vision.

SWIMMING LEGS
Flattened and fringed with hair, the two pairs of hind legs propel the toe-biter through the water.

ROSTRUM
The toe-biter uses this strong, sharp "beak" to inject venom and digestive juices into prey. It's hollow, letting the bug suck up the victim's insides.

GRASPING LEGS
The powerful front legs are used to seize prey.

The toe-biter is the biggest and meanest bug in freshwater. Fish, insects, and even small waterbirds have no defense against this huge, fearless predator. Once a hungry toe-biter has a victim in its grasp, it plunges its hollow, needlelike mouthparts into its body and injects a cocktail of paralyzing venom and digestive juices.

Sometimes, the toe-biter lives up to its name and grabs the toes of an unwary human—the victim will think twice before dipping his or her toes into the water again.

HOW BIG IS IT?

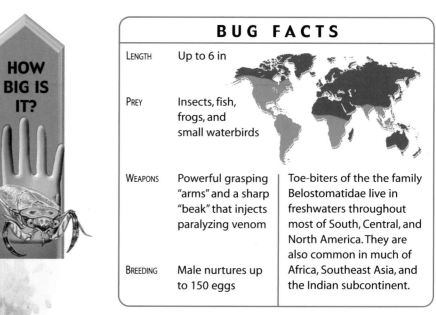

BUG FACTS

LENGTH	Up to 6 in	
PREY	Insects, fish, frogs, and small waterbirds	
WEAPONS	Powerful grasping "arms" and a sharp "beak" that injects paralyzing venom	Toe-biters of the the family Belostomatidae live in freshwaters throughout most of South, Central, and North America. They are also common in much of Africa, Southeast Asia, and the Indian subcontinent.
BREEDING	Male nurtures up to 150 eggs	

A boy fishing on a hot day dangles his bare feet in the water. He wriggles his toes in pleasure. The wriggling movement attracts a hungry toe-biter.

1

Hoping for a juicy meal, the toe-biter swims closer and grabs the boy's foot. Feeling a sudden stab of pain, the boy jerks his foot out of the water. The toe-biter is still attached.

2

Did You Know?

● Toe-biters sometimes take to the air and, despite their size, they fly well. Like moths, they are drawn to streetlights at night, a habit that has earned them the name "electric light bugs."

● Some male toe-biters attract females by using their bodies to generate low-frequency ripples on the water's surface. Unfortunately, these ripples can attract hungry fishing spiders instead.

● Toe-biters often attack and eat their own kind. In fact, most young toe-biters fall victim to bigger toe-biters and other water predators.

● In some Asian countries, such as Thailand and China, people eat water bugs as a delicacy. The bugs are a vital ingredient of a spicy Thai sauce called *namphala*.

● Some toe-biters pretend to be dead when first picked up by humans, then attack the hand that is holding them.

SPITTLEBUG
Latin name: Family Cercopidae

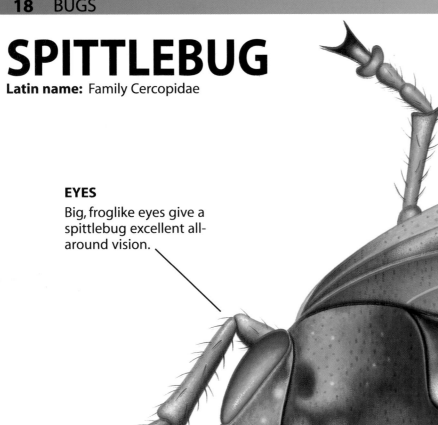

WINGS
The tough forewings form a protective shield, totally covering the body.

EYES
Big, froglike eyes give a spittlebug excellent all-around vision.

COLOR
Most spittlebugs are dull green or brown to blend in with the surrounding vegetation. Some species are brightly colored to warn birds and other predators that they taste awful.

HEAD
Like most bugs, a spittlebug keeps its mouthparts folded away under its body when it isn't feeding.

LEGS
Tiny leg-hairs help the bug sense surface vibrations. Spines on the back legs provide extra grip before a leap.

A young spittlebug has one of the weirdest survival techniques in the entire animal world. It disguises itself from predators by blowing a mass of long-lasting bubbles.

It creates the froth by secreting a waxy substance and loads of watery waste. The foam covers the nymph completely. To stop itself from drowning, the nymph pokes the water-repellent tip of its abdomen through the froth to suck up air.

HOW BIG IS IT?

Actual Size

An aphid infestation is irresistible to a ladybug. She grabs bug after plump bug with her long jaws. She's so busy eating she totally ignores the frothy mass that covers an adjoining stem.

1

By covering itself in a coat of foam, a spittlebug nymph makes itself invisible. The strategy works and the hungry ladybug never notices the tasty meal right next to it.

2

BUG FACTS

LENGTH	$1/5$–$4/5$ in, depending on species	
DIET	Plant sap	
DEFENSES	Nymph hides itself inside a bubble of foam; adult relies on jumping reflexes	Between 2,500 and 3,000 species of spittlebug live throughout the world, except for the coldest regions. They inhabit all kinds of well-vegetated habitats, from scrub and woodlands to gardens and meadows.
LIFESPAN	About 6 months	

Did You Know?

● In Africa, spittlebugs sometimes occur in such numbers and produce so much spittle that it is said to drip from the branches of trees like rain.

● Some species of spittlebug are real pests and cause serious damage with their toxic saliva, leaving brown lesions on the plant leaves, known as "spittlebug blight." In Trinidad they are notorious for destroying sugarcane; in other places they harm pine and willow trees with their activities.

● Some ants have grown wise to this bugs' cover, and after using the spit as a building material, they prey on the nymphs inside.

● An adult male spittlebug wards off rival males and attracts mates by making clicking noises. He produces these sounds with stiff membranes known as tymbals, located on each side of his first abdominal segment. Flexing his muscles, he clicks the membranes in and out, and special air sacs amplify the resulting sounds.

CICADA

Latin name: Family Cicadidae

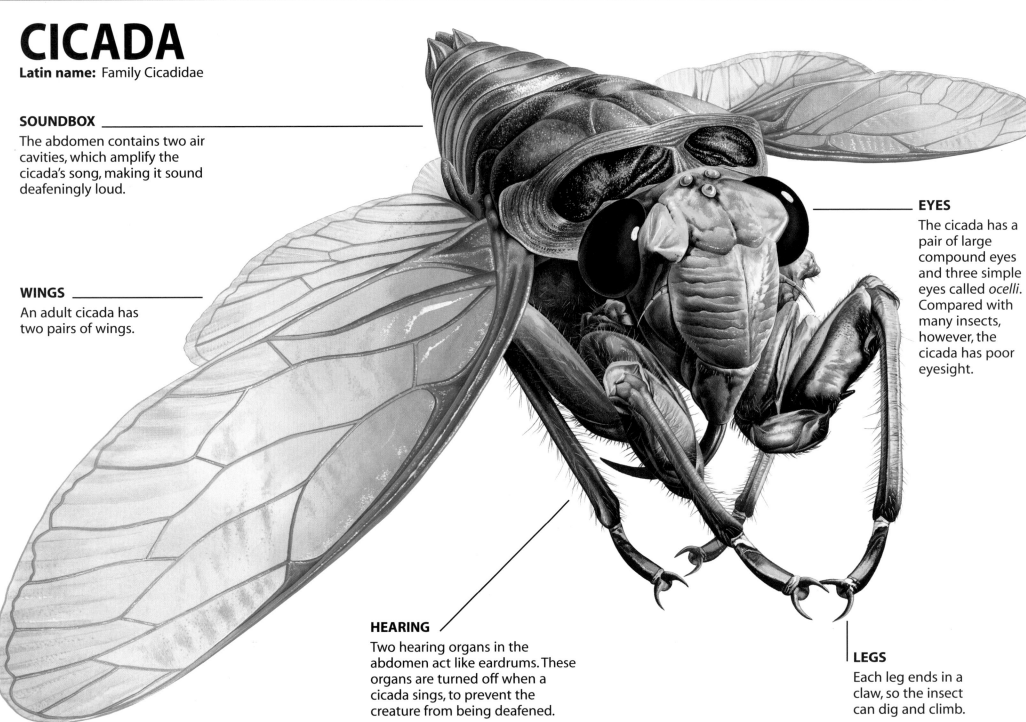

SOUNDBOX

The abdomen contains two air cavities, which amplify the cicada's song, making it sound deafeningly loud.

WINGS

An adult cicada has two pairs of wings.

EYES

The cicada has a pair of large compound eyes and three simple eyes called *ocelli*. Compared with many insects, however, the cicada has poor eyesight.

HEARING

Two hearing organs in the abdomen act like eardrums. These organs are turned off when a cicada sings, to prevent the creature from being deafened.

LEGS

Each leg ends in a claw, so the insect can dig and climb.

Hidden deep undergound, a cicada nymph spends years drinking sap from tree roots in safety. Then, responding to a mysterious inner clock, it leaves its secure burrow, climbs the nearest tree, and turns into a buzzing, chirruping adult. In most of the world's warmer countries, a stroll in the sun is almost always accompanied by the constant, ear-ringing calls of adult cicadas that have emerged in plaguelike swarms.

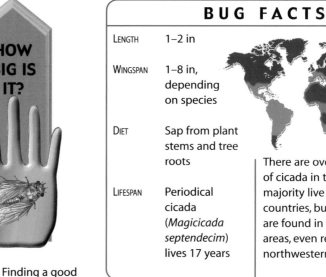

HOW BIG IS IT?

1 After digging its way out of the soil, a cicada nymph scrambles up a tree trunk, gripping the bark with its tiny claws.

2 Finding a good hiding place high in the tree, the nymph begins to shed its skin. A split appears in its outer covering, which slowly opens to reveal the adult cicada inside.

3 Breaking free of its old skin, the newly emerged adult basks in the sunshine. The adult spends up to six days hardening its new wings and body before it is ready to begin courtship.

BUG FACTS

LENGTH	1–2 in
WINGSPAN	1–8 in, depending on species
DIET	Sap from plant stems and tree roots
LIFESPAN	Periodical cicada (*Magicicada septendecim*) lives 17 years

There are over 1,500 species of cicada in the world. The majority live in tropical countries, but a few are found in more temperate areas, even reaching as far as northwestern Europe.

Did You Know?

● Adult cicadas drink so much tree sap to get the nutrients they need that droplets of watery waste expelled from their bodies fall like rain from the trees they occupy.

● Cicadas are among the biggest insects, yet are closely related to some of the smallest, such as aphids.

● The giant Malaysian empress cicada (*Pomponia imperatoria*) has the biggest wingspan, at 8 inches.

● The periodical cicada of North America has a 17-year life cycle in the north of its range and a 13-year life cycle in the south.

● Some cicadas become infected with a fungus that causes the rear of the abdomen to break off, revealing a chalky mass of spores.

● A wasp, *Sphecius speciosus*, paralyzes adult cicadas and fills its nests with their bodies to provide food for its growing larvae.

BEDBUG

Latin name: *Cimex lectularius*

ANTENNAS
Sensitive antennas easily detect the scent and heat of a warm body.

EYES
Small, compound eyes are used mainly to check it is dark enough to go in search of sleeping victims.

FEET
Each foot is equipped with two tiny hooks. This helps the bedbug grip rough surfaces as it climbs around.

PROBOSCIS
The needlelike mouthparts are protected by a tough sheath. When the bedbug isn't feeding, it folds the whole arrangement under its body.

ABDOMEN
When the bedbug is looking for a meal, its abdomen is brown, crinkly, and wafer-thin. As the bug feeds, it becomes bloated and crimson with blood.

A miniature, creeping vampire, a bedbug can lie dormant in a cool crevice for more than a year. Sneaking out in the dead of night, the bedbug feasts on the warm blood of human victims while they sleep. Drinking more than five times its own weight in blood, the bedbug blows up like a balloon as it feeds.

Waddling back into hiding, the bug can take several days to digest its meal. A bug's favorite retreats are within easy reach of its food supply: in the seams of mattresses and the joints of timber bed frames.

HOW BIG IS IT?

x5

Sensing the heat of a sleeping human, the bedbug crawls onto the exposed flesh of the victim's neck. It grips with tiny hooked feet.

1

1

2

3

BUG FACTS

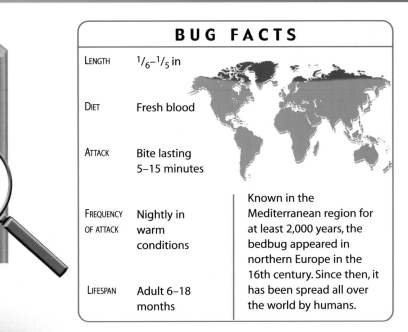

LENGTH	$^1/_6$–$^1/_5$ in
DIET	Fresh blood
ATTACK	Bite lasting 5–15 minutes
FREQUENCY OF ATTACK	Nightly in warm conditions
LIFESPAN	Adult 6–18 months

Known in the Mediterranean region for at least 2,000 years, the bedbug appeared in northern Europe in the 16th century. Since then, it has been spread all over the world by humans.

2

The bedbug extracts blood the same way a doctor does, using a hypodermic needle. It injects saliva to stop the blood from clotting.

3

The bedbug's gut inflates rapidly, turning the bug's body dark purple. Bacteria in the bedbug's digestive system turn some of the blood meal into vital vitamins.

Did You Know?

● The bedbug has a gland under its body that produces an oily liquid when it is disturbed. This has an odor similar to the smell of raspberries, and it is possible to detect an infested house by the smell.

● In the past, crushed bedbugs were often used in folk remedies for infected wounds. Recent tests have found that their blood contains a substance that kills bacteria.

● Other common names for the bedbug include the wall louse, crimson rambler, or mahogany flat.

● Bulgarian peasants used to try to protect themselves from bedbugs by putting runner-bean leaves around their beds—maybe the hairs on the leaves trapped the bugs.

BUTTERFLY BUG

Latin name: Family Flatidae

EYES
The weak eyes are only able to tell whether it is night or day.

WAX "TAIL"
The long streamers of wax help disguise the nymph as moss or lichen growing on a plant.

BODY
The body of the nymph is very like that of an adult butterfly bug. But it has no wings.

ANTENNAS
Short and stubby, the antennas help the bug examine its immediate environment.

LEGS
As well as for moving, the bug uses its legs for grooming and for grasping its partner during mating.

Small and vulnerable, these sap-drinking butterfly bug nymphs should make a tasty snack for a variety of creatures. But by using a clever mixture of disguise and surprise, they manage to keep their multitude of enemies at bay. As the nymphs cluster together, the waxy tendrils and fibers on their bodies form a protective disguise, cunningly resembling clumps of lichen or moss.

HOW BIG IS IT?

Actual Size

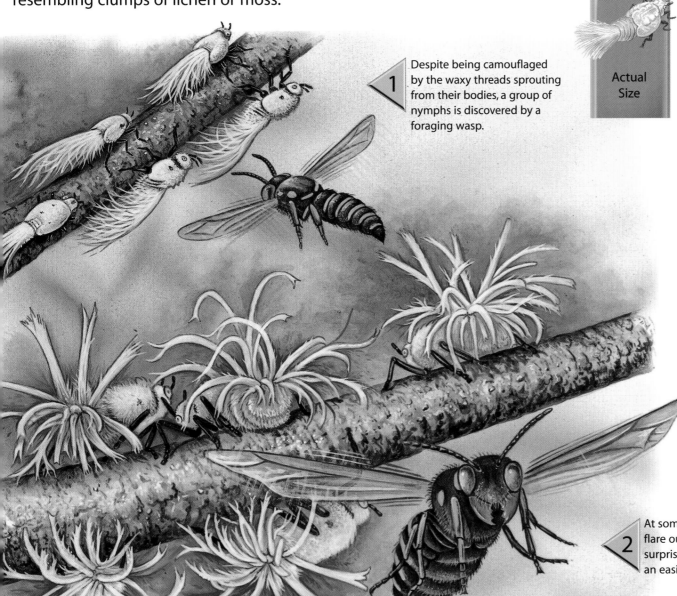

1 Despite being camouflaged by the waxy threads sprouting from their bodies, a group of nymphs is discovered by a foraging wasp.

2 At some secret signal, the nymphs flare out their "tails." The wasp is surprised and backs off in search of an easier target.

BUG FACTS

SPECIES	Over 1,000
LENGTH	Up to 1 in
LIFESTYLE	Lives on plants in groups for safety
DIET	Plant sap
WEAPONS	None
DEFENSES	Nymph uses camouflage and shock tactics; adult relies on camouflage
LIFESPAN	A few months as both a nymph and an adult

Butterfly bugs are found virtually worldwide, but most species live in tropical regions. Tropical species are usually more brightly colored than those living in temperate areas.

Did You Know?

● Male and female butterfly bugs are often quite different colors. In the past, many scientists classed the two sexes of the same type of bug as completely different species!

● The waxy tufts of butterfly bug nymphs not only protect them from enemies, they also trap a layer of air that insulates the insects from the cold at night and in bad weather.

● Relatives of butterfly bugs called lac insects (family Kerriidae) produce a waxy resin that people turn into a substance called shellac. This is the basis of the French polish used on furniture. It was also once used to make gramophone records, before the invention of vinyl.

PEANUT BUG

Latin name: *Fulgoridae laternaria*

HIND WINGS
Usually covered by the forewings, these are brightly colored with defensive eyespots.

FOREWINGS
The forewings are colored to match the bug's preferred habitat, providing almost perfect camouflage.

HEAD
Looking like an unshelled peanut, the bug's head is virtually hollow. The extension is probably a defensive device. It can also be bashed against a tree to produce a drumming sound.

LEGS
Strong legs tipped with long, sharp claws help the bug cling to trees.

EYES
Small, compound eyes are good at spotting movement.

Any creature disturbing a peanut bug as it sucks up plant sap is in for a shock. At first glance its head looks like a tiny alligator. And if that isn't enough to scare anyone, the bug has a range of other defensive tricks.

This bizarrely shaped bug is a master of defense and deception. It has carefully camouflaged forewings and dramatic defensive headspots on its hind wings. Along with its weird hollow head and noxious sprays to frighten off its enemies, the peanut bug has many other tricks at its disposal to scare away potential predators.

HOW BIG IS IT?

BUG FACTS

LENGTH	Varies from $1/3$–6 in depending on the species
WINGSPAN	$4/5$–12 in
HEAD	Up to 2 in long
DIET	Nutrient-rich plant juices
LIFESPAN	1–2 years

Peanut bugs are a variety of lantern bug. These live in tropical forests around the world, in Africa, Asia, and Australia. But the greatest variety of lantern bug species is found in Central and South America.

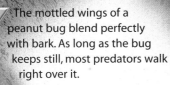

1 The mottled wings of a peanut bug blend perfectly with bark. As long as the bug keeps still, most predators walk right over it.

If grabbed or knocked to the ground, the bug opens its upper wings to reveal orange spots beneath. These look like the staring eyes of an owl. Few predators risk attacking in case they end up as lunch themselves.

2

3 If a peanut bug is spotted on the move, it often releases a spray of noxious chemicals. These smell almost as bad as a skunk. Few predators want to swallow such a foul-smelling meal.

4 If a predator persists, the peanut bug knocks its hollow head against a hard surface, making a loud drumming sound. This can confuse a predator just long enough for the bug to escape.

Did You Know?

● It may be that baby caiman (a type of alligator) are predators of animals that feed on peanut bugs, and their disguise acts as a deterrent.

● Male peanut bugs attract mates by rapidly banging their abdomens against tree trunks. Females hear this mating call and home in on the sound.

● Peanut bugs are a particular species of lantern bug. Some types of lantern bug are attacked by caterpillars of a type of burnet moth. Up to 3000 of these needle-nosed creatures may crawl under the bug's wings, plunging their sharp mouthparts into its body to suck out its insides.

● Some close relatives of the peanut bug carry bacteria in their guts that they unknowingly vomit into a plant when they feed. These multiply rapidly inside the plant, consuming up to 100 times their own body weight of its vital fluids daily. An infected plant soon starves to death. Crops of coffee and sugarcane can be devastated by this type of killer bacteria.

TOAD BUG

Latin name: Family Gelastocoridae

FORELEGS
These are modified for grasping prey, with double claws at the tip.

BODY
Squat and rounded, the body is yellowish to dark brown. Rough wingcases cover the upper surface.

EYES
The big eyes bulge outward and upward, like those of a toad. These give the toad bug excellent vision as it stalks prey across mud.

HEAD
The wide, flat head fits snugly against the body. The beaklike mouthparts are tucked away underneath.

ANTENNAS
The bug has unusually short antennas compared with others of its kind. They are so tiny that they are hidden by the body when the bug is viewed from above.

HIND LEGS
Long, slender hind legs provide the power for the bug to make impressive leaps across the ground.

Down at the water's edge, hidden in the mud, lurks a strangely familiar-looking bug. Given its large eyes, rough skin, and hopping habits, it is easy to see how the toad bug got its name. This athletic killer claims its prey with a leap and a lightning stab. Being much smaller than a real toad, the bug can't snap up insects whole. Instead it's armed with piercing mouthparts, designed for sucking out a victim's body contents.

HOW BIG IS IT?

Actual Size

BUG FACTS

SPECIES	About 150 known species in two genera: *Gelastocoris* and *Nerthra*	
LENGTH	$1/4$–$1/2$in	
PREY	Insects and other small organisms	Toad bugs are common in much of North America, all of Central and South America, sub-Saharan Africa, southern Asia, and Australasia, but seem to be absent in temperate Eurasia.
WEAPONS	Grasping forelegs, piercing mouthparts, and powerful digestive enzymes	
TACTICS	Leaps onto prey and pins it to the ground	
LIFESPAN	Unknown	

△ **1**
A fly lands close to a pond, not realizing that the large "pebble" nearby is the lumpy body of a toad bug. Moving carefully, the toad bug sneaks close to the unsuspecting fly.

2 ◁
Springing suddenly into the air, the toad bug jumps on top of its victim. It stabs its beak into the fly's body and pumps in a stream of saliva, rapidly turning the fly's insides into liquid. It sucks up the liquid hungrily.

Did You Know?

● Toad bugs belonging to the genus *Gelastocoris* possess scent glands that secrete an unpleasant substance designed to deter would-be predators. The glands open on the back of the thorax and special valves control the release of scent.

● A toad bug produces tiny oval eggs, and if these are viewed under a microscope, a fine hexagonal pattern can be seen on the surface. The area within each hexagon is densely perforated by minute pores.

● Toad bug nymphs resemble the adults in overall structure, although their body parts are differently proportioned and their wings do not develop fully until the final molt.

WATER STRIDER

Latin name: *Gerris* species

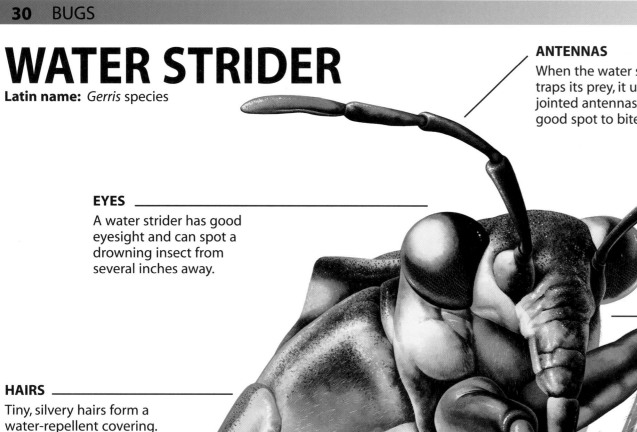

ANTENNAS

When the water strider traps its prey, it uses its jointed antennas to find a good spot to bite.

EYES

A water strider has good eyesight and can spot a drowning insect from several inches away.

HAIRS

Tiny, silvery hairs form a water-repellent covering. This stops the insect from sinking into the water.

PROBOSCIS

The water strider uses this to stab into a victim's body, then to pump in digestive fluids, and finally to suck out the resulting goo.

MIDDLE LEGS

Long middle legs stick out sideways like oars. These propel the water strider swiftly across the water's surface.

FEET

The water strider's feet never break through the water's surface.

t looks fragile but the water strider (also called a water skimmer) is a nasty little killer with a clever trick. It can walk on water, preying on the flying insects that crash-land on its home pond.

The water strider balances on the surface of the water, its sensitive feet quickly picking up vibrations made by the struggling insects. It can then whiz along the top of the pond, covering a yard in a second, using a second pair of legs as oars and steering with its hind legs.

HOW BIG IS IT?

Actual Size

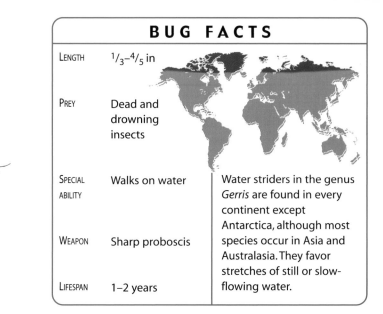

BUG FACTS

LENGTH	$1/3$–$4/5$ in	
PREY	Dead and drowning insects	
SPECIAL ABILITY	Walks on water	Water striders in the genus *Gerris* are found in every continent except Antarctica, although most species occur in Asia and Australasia. They favor stretches of still or slow-flowing water.
WEAPON	Sharp proboscis	
LIFESPAN	1–2 years	

2

Darting closer, the agile predator stabs deeply into the moth's body. It injects a strong dissolving liquid. As it sucks up the resulting soup, more water striders move in to join the banquet.

1

A forester moth swoops too close to a pond and crash-lands on the surface. A nearby water strider notices its feeble struggles and glides in for a kill.

Did You Know?

● In South Africa the water strider is called the waterloper.

● Household detergents and other pollutants in water destroy the surface tension. If this occurs, water striders sink and drown.

● Many fish thrive on insects trapped on the water's surface, but they rarely eat water striders, whose feet leave such tiny, widely spaced impressions on the water that they are virtually invisible from below.

● A population of water striders may contain adults with or without wings. It is thought that the winged individuals use them to fly to new waters if their home stretch becomes overcrowded or polluted.

● Some water striders from the family Gerridae hunt on the surface of the open ocean. They are the only insects to be found in this environment.

TREEHOPPER

Latin name: Family Membracidae

PRONOTUM

A tough shell-like material, called cuticle, forms the pronotum. In some species, this looks like an open-jawed ant, which can frighten away predators.

WINGS

These are transparent, and are often almost hidden by the huge pronotum.

MOUTHPARTS

When the treehopper isn't feeding, it folds its "beak" under its body.

These strange-looking bugs often have such outrageous growths on their backs, it's surprising they can hop or fly at all. The unwieldy growths are a part of an elaborate defense system.

Treehoppers use various disguises to escape predators, and some species can produce toxic secretions. Other types of treehopper form a close relationship with ants, who help protect them from danger.

HOW BIG IS IT?

x2

BUG FACTS

LENGTH	Up to $1/2$ in, depending on species	
DIET	Plant sap	
LIFESTYLE	Lives on trees, shrubs, and grasses, often gathering in large groups	Nearly 2,500 species of treehopper are found worldwide, the most bizarre and colorful coming from tropical regions. Many more undiscovered species probably exist in remote areas of rain forest.
LIFESPAN	Up to 2 years	

Treehoppers, such as *Sphongophorus guerini* (1) of Trinidad, look remarkably like the thorns of a plant, especially when several line up along a branch or stem. Other treehopper species, such as *Umbonia spinosa* (2) of Peru, are brightly colored to warn birds and other predators that they taste unpleasant. And species such as *Gelastogonia erthropus* (3), from Brazil, obtain protection from ants by feeding them with honeydew.

Did You Know?

● Although treehoppers feed on plants, some people have reported being "bitten" by them. This isn't strictly true, as treehoppers cannot bite. However, they may occasionally stab through someone's skin with their pointed mouthparts in an attempt to suck up moisture.

● The females of some treehopper species lay their eggs in a huge pile and stand guard in a circle around the edge. They release unpleasant chemicals from their abdomen as a warning to predators, and defend the eggs by fanning their wings vigorously, making loud buzzing noises or rapid movements, and even by head-butting attackers.

● Some treehoppers, such as the American buffalo treehopper, are considered pests because of the damage they do to fruit trees. The female of this species slits the bark of an apple tree with her sharp ovipositor (egg-laying tube) and inserts her eggs underneath the bark, often resulting in the death of the tree.

DAMSEL BUG

Latin name: Family Nabidae

WINGS
The wings of many damsel bugs are only partially formed. The bugs generally prefer to walk.

EYES
Large compound eyes spot the slightest movement.

ANTENNAS
The long antennas are equipped with sensitive receptors.

ROSTRUM
A protective rostrum covers the needlelike mouthparts. These can be pulled out of the way when the bug feeds.

RAPTORIAL LEGS
The strong, grasping front legs are known as raptorial legs. They can hold far larger insects in their grip.

STYLETS
The rostrum covers four thin mouthparts called stylets. These slice through skin and suck up the bug's liquid food.

The empty husks of insects littering the leaves may be the only evidence that a damsel bug is around. This tiny assassin is the deadly enemy of garden aphids, caterpillars, and beetle grubs. In fact, there are not many insects, large or small, that don't feature on a damsel bug menu.

These sneaky little killers think nothing of creeping up on prey and stabbing them in the back with their long, sharp mouths. Wherever insects are feeding, a damsel bug is sure to be lurking close at hand.

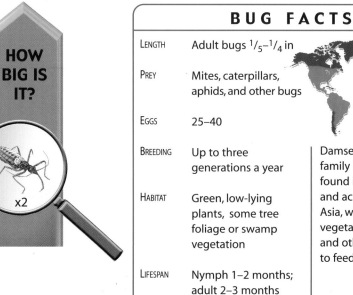

HOW BIG IS IT?

x2

BUG FACTS

LENGTH	Adult bugs $1/5$–$1/4$ in	
PREY	Mites, caterpillars, aphids, and other bugs	
EGGS	25–40	
BREEDING	Up to three generations a year	Damsel bugs in the family Nabidae are found in the Americas and across Europe and Asia, wherever there is vegetation to hide in and other invertebrates to feed on.
HABITAT	Green, low-lying plants, some tree foliage or swamp vegetation	
LIFESPAN	Nymph 1–2 months; adult 2–3 months	

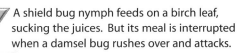

1 A shield bug nymph feeds on a birch leaf, sucking the juices. But its meal is interrupted when a damsel bug rushes over and attacks.

2 The damsel bug grabs the nymph with its front legs and flips its victim over. It sinks its sharp snout deep into a chink in the nymph's armor.

Did You Know?

● A male damsel bug has sharp reproductive organs, which he uses to pierce the female's tough body casing during mating. He injects his sperm directly into her body cavity, and they are transported to her eggs in her body fluids—a process known as traumatic insemination.

● Sometimes, damsel bugs and their relatives smear the sticky sap from plants onto their legs, which helps them keep a grip on struggling prey.

● Big damsel bugs happily turn to cannibalism if the chance arises, stabbing any smaller damsel bugs.

● There are about 400 damsel bug species. All of them are predators.

WATER SCORPION

Latin name: *Nepidae* species

SIPHON

The breathing tube is made up of two long grooved halves hooked together with tiny hairs. The bug thrusts this rigid "snorkel" up through the surface film of the water to take in air.

LIMBS

The front pair of limbs is elongated for snatching prey. The middle and hind legs are used for walking along the bottom or climbing over plants.

ABDOMEN

Sensory organs allow the water scorpion to measure water pressure. This way, the bug can tell which way is up and find its way to the surface.

MOUTHPARTS

The daggerlike "beak" can pierce prey and even give humans a nasty nip. The water scorpion also uses its "beak" to inject digestive juices into prey and then suck out the dissolved nutrients.

Cloaked in drab brown armor, the water scorpion loiters in ponds and ditches. It uses classic ambush techniques to capture its prey: perfect camouflage combined with a lightning-fast strike. Only then does it show the strength of its pincers, which overpower its prey in seconds. The sharp tip of its beaklike mouthparts punches through fish scales or the shell of insect bodies as efficiently as a sharp knife.

Tadpoles, small fish, and insect larvae, as well as the adults and nymphs of other water bug species, are all potential victims.

HOW BIG IS IT?

Actual Size

BUG FACTS

LENGTH OF BODY	Male $^3/_5$–$^5/_7$ in; female $^4/_5$–1 in
LENGTH OF SIPHON	$^1/_3$–$^1/_2$ in
DIET	Small fish and tadpoles and insects and their larvae
LIFECYCLE	Eggs laid April–May; adults appear in August and hibernate
HUNTING METHOD	Captures prey in forelegs; then, like a spider, it injects enzymes into prey to liquefy internal tissues

Although found virtually worldwide, water scorpions of the *Nepidae* species are most numerous in tropical regions and very scarce in Australasia and cold regions. The European species, *Nepa cinerea*, occurs through Europe as far east as the Urals, and in North Africa.

1 Clinging upside down to the pond vegetation, a water scorpion thrusts its long breathing tube up toward the air. Air flows into the cavity beneath the bug's shell. The bug waits in ambush for prey.

2 As soon as a small fish swims within range, the water scorpion strikes as quick as a flash. It grabs the fish in the firm grip of its scythelike forelegs and pulls it in toward its stabbing jaws.

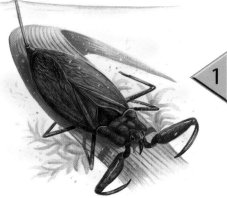

3 The water scorpion devours its helpless prey, tearing at the fish's flesh. It then injects a deadly dose of venomous saliva, which turns the fish's innards to a runny soup. The water scorpion sucks up the fish juices.

Did You Know?

● The water scorpion can actually hang by its siphon from the surface film of the water.

● If disturbed, this inconspicuous little bug may play dead until danger has passed.

● Although it is classed as a nonswimmer, the water scorpion can scull along by moving its forelegs up and down and kicking with its middle and hind legs.

● The female water scorpion uses her siphon for laying eggs. The eggs are shaped rather like a tiny jellyfish. Each has seven long, dangling projections by which it is attached to water plants.

STINK BUG

Latin name: Family Pentatomidae

WINGS
The bug has two pairs of wings. The front pair fold on top of the back pair.

ARMOR
An armored shield, called the pronotum, covers the front part of the bug's body.

ANTENNAS
These long feelers help the bug find food and mates by touch and taste.

ABDOMEN
The flattened body contains most of the bug's vital organs.

EYES
The adult bug has compound eyes that react to movement.

LEGS
These tuck neatly under the body when the bug flattens itself against a leaf or twig.

PROBOSCIS
Protected by a fleshy sheath, this tube is used for sucking up food. It's folded under the body when not in use.

This colorful little creature is a tempting snack for a bird, so the moment it feels threatened, it gives off a foul smell to warn that it tastes revolting, too. With its body armor and cunning use of color, the stink bug is well equipped to survive in a hostile world.

Killer stink bugs keep things simple. Targeting defenseless, slow-moving grubs, they have no need of craftily camouflaged traps to catch their prey. Instead, they just walk up to it and start eating.

HOW BIG IS IT?

Actual Size

BUG FACTS

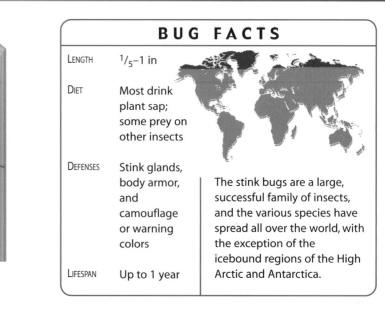

LENGTH	$1/5$–1 in
DIET	Most drink plant sap; some prey on other insects
DEFENSES	Stink glands, body armor, and camouflage or warning colors
LIFESPAN	Up to 1 year

The stink bugs are a large, successful family of insects, and the various species have spread all over the world, with the exception of the icebound regions of the High Arctic and Antarctica.

1 High in the branches of a tree, a stink bug finds a fat caterpillar crawling sluggishly across a leaf.

2 The bug plunges its proboscis into the caterpillar, injecting paralyzing, digestive saliva. The grub wriggles feebly as the bug starts sucking out its insides. Delicious!

Did You Know?

● There are at least 5,000 species of stink bug in the Pentatomidae family—not to mention quite a few more in closely related families.

● When stink bugs crawl over wild blackberries and bilberries, they often smear them with the smelly secretions from their stink glands—which is why these fruits sometimes leave an unpleasant taste in the mouth.

● Compared with other insects, female stink bugs are unusually attentive mothers, diligently guarding their eggs and young until they are old enough to fend for themselves.

● The defensive scent of a stink bug occasionally works against it, by attracting a parasitic fly that lays an egg on the bug's body. On hatching, the larva (grub) of the fly burrows into the bug and eats it alive.

● In some species of stink bug, the nymphs are camouflaged, while the adults have bold warning colors.

AMBUSH BUG

Latin name: Family Phymatidae

BODY

Many species have spiky projections on their body, for camouflage or as defensive armor.

WINGS

An ambush bug has two pairs of wings but isn't a strong flyer. It takes to the air to flee from danger or to find a flower.

MOUTHPARTS

The bug retracts its piercing mouthparts when waiting in ambush. It extends them only when it has a victim.

FRONT LEGS

Strong muscles clamp the large legs around a victim's body until the ambush bug has eaten its fill.

I t may be an aggressive predator, but the ambush bug doesn't waste energy chasing after prey. It sits tight, usually on a flower, until the unwary insect arrives and serves itself for dinner. By the time an insect sees the ambush bug move, it's too late.

This lightning-quick hunter waits stock-still until a victim is near, then snatches it up in the blink of an eye. Once it has grabbed its prey, the ambush bug injects a digestive saliva deep into its body. Then it sucks out the insides. It won't let go until it has sucked the insect dry.

HOW BIG IS IT?

Actual Size

B U G   F A C T S

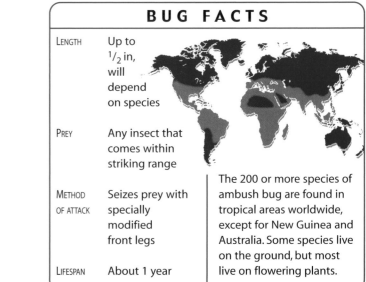

Length	Up to 1/2 in, will depend on species	
Prey	Any insect that comes within striking range	
Method of attack	Seizes prey with specially modified front legs	
Lifespan	About 1 year	

The 200 or more species of ambush bug are found in tropical areas worldwide, except for New Guinea and Australia. Some species live on the ground, but most live on flowering plants.

1 An ambush bug sits motionless on a flower as a hoverfly hovers in front of the bloom. The fly is alert to the slightest sign of danger, but the bug stays as still as a statue.

2 The fly lands to feed, and the bug pounces. The fly struggles hard to escape, but the bug's grip is simply too strong.

Did You Know?

● A newly hatched ambush bug is called a nymph. When it emerges from its egg, it's a miniature version of its parents, except for the wings, which start off as tiny projections called buds. The nymph sheds its hard exoskeleton ("skin") several times as it grows, before becoming a fully formed adult.

● "Ambush Bug" was a humorous cartoon character in the USA in the 1980s. Raised by a television set, he had special electronic powers and could transport himself anywhere.

● Ambush bugs are true bugs, which all have two pairs of wings and piercing, sucking mouthparts. Most of the 30,000 or so species of true bugs feed on plant juices but some, such as ambush and assassin bugs, are predators, while others are bloodsucking parasites.

● Ambush bugs have reportedly been seen catching bees by seizing their long tongues as they feed.

CHAGAS BUG

Latin name: *Triatoma, Panstrongylus,* and *Rhodnius* species

ANTENNAS

The segmented antennas are packed with sensors to help the Chagas bug locate its next victim.

ABDOMEN

The bug's abdomen (body) contains its gut. This is where the microbes that cause Chagas' disease develop.

LEGS

After a meal of blood, the bug is far too heavy to fly far. Luckily, long legs give the Chagas bug a good turn of speed.

BEAK

The bug usually carries its long, piercing "beak" folded beneath its body. It unfolds it only when it needs to eat.

EYES

The Chagas bug sees well with its compound eyes. But it's a night hunter and usually locates its victims by scent.

Tiptoeing across a victim's face, the Chagas bug often makes for the soft skin of the mouth and eyes. It inserts its feeding tube under the skin, probing for a blood vessel. It may then feed for up to 20 minutes, taking up to ten times its own weight in blood.

As if that wasn't nasty enough, it often defecates on the skin. This excrement may contains parasites that cause disease. This bloodsucking bug plagues the people of villages and towns in Central and South America, spreading an infection known as Chagas' disease.

HOW BIG IS IT?

Actual Size

1

A woman sleeps peacefully, unaware of the hungry Chagas bug creeping over her face.

Drilling painlessly into her skin, the bug settles down to a meal of blood. As it feeds, it dumps a gutful of infected excrement.

2

When the woman wakes, she rubs her itching face. The deadly microbes are rubbed into the bite wound and around her eye.

3

BUG FACTS

LENGTH	4/5 in	Triatomine bugs infected with Chagas' disease live in most of Central and South America. The "domestic" species have adapted almost exclusively to places of human habitation, while the "sylvatic" species live in various outdoor habitats, from the crowns of palm trees to animal burrows and birds' nests. Some triatomines also occur in the southwestern USA, but are less likely to pass on the infection.
DIET	Fresh blood	
ATTACK	Single bite per insect	
INFECTION	*Trypanosoma cruzi*, the Chagas' disease organism	
LIFESPAN	1 year or more	

Did You Know?

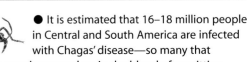

● It is estimated that 16–18 million people in Central and South America are infected with Chagas' disease—so many that microbes may be passed on in the blood of unwitting donors and transmitted by transfusion.

● Scientists once collected more than 7,000 Chagas bugs from just one small hut in South America.

● In some areas of Mexico, Chagas' disease is passed on when people use triatomine bugs in love potions or even eat them covered in hot sauce. Others catch the disease by using the bug's feces as a cure for warts.

● From his memoirs, we now know that the famous naturalist Charles Darwin caught Chagas' disease in 1835. His symptoms baffled doctors, but he continued to suffer them until he died 47 years later.

● Chagas' disease is named after Carlos Chagas, a Brazilian doctor who discovered how it was spread in 1909.

Beetles

Beetles belong to the insect family called Coleopotera. This name comes from the Greek word for "sheath-winged." This means that their front set of wings forms a hard cover or sheath to protect the back set of wings.

Some beetles can grow very large. One of the biggest beetles of all is the Hercules beetle, which lives in the South American rain forest. The Hercules beetle is named after the big, strong hero of Greek myth and can grow up to seven inches in length—as big as a rat! The tiniest beetle is thirty times smaller, only a faction of an inch long.

Beetles make up around half of all the animals on Earth. About 370,000 species or families of beetles are known to scientists, but there are still many more to be found. Centuries ago, in ancient Egypt, the brightly colored scarab, or dung beetle, was treated as a god. The Egyptians believed it was a sign that people could come back to life after death.

Beetles live on land and in water and feed on almost anything that can be eaten. The Colorado beetle, for instance, eats potatoes. The deathwatch beetle eats wood. Both are called "pests" because they are very destructive. Other beetles are much more helpful. For example, the dung beetle's diet may not seem very pleasant to us but it does help to recycle all those smelly animal droppings.

HARLEQUIN BEETLE

Latin name: *Acrocinus longimanus*

WINGCASES
When the beetle flies, its hard wingcases move forward, out of the way of the long wings.

ANTENNAS
The long, backward-curving antennas are covered in sensory hairs and scent-detecting cells.

FORELEGS
Tiny toothlike projections cover the long forelegs.

SPINES
Spines on the body may deter enemies from attacking.

CLAWS
These can find a hold on even the smoothest bark.

PADS
Hairy pads on the bottom of the beetle's feet give extra grip on leaves, twigs, and branches.

EYES
These are unusually large to make the most of the dim light deep in the forest.

This tropical American giant looks as colorful and clumsy as a clown. However, its bold patterning actually hides it from predators on tropical trees mottled with fungus and lichen. The harlequin beetle starts life as a wood-munching grub that can lay waste to whole trees. The grub gobbles many times its own body weight in food as it chews its way around a tree trunk, growing fatter and fatter.

HOW BIG IS IT?

BUG FACTS

LENGTH	Body up to 4 in; antennas up to 4 3/4 in; forelegs 5 in or more (longer on male than female)	The harlequin beetle is found in tropical forests in southern Mexico, most of Central America, and much of South America, throughout the Amazon Basin and south to northern Argentina. It is also found on the Caribbean islands of Trinidad and Barbados. In places it is known as the *mouche bagasse*, or jack-tree borer, due to its liking for bagasse and jackfruit trees.
DIET	Larva eats wood; adult eats mainly tree sap	
LIFESPAN	Unknown	

GREEDY GRUBS

The female beetle uses her powerful jaws to make a hole in a tree trunk, then lays 15 to 20 eggs in it. About ten days later, the grubs hatch. In the next seven or eight months, the grubs eat out spiraling tunnels through the wood. Each grub then carves out a chamber and seals itself in. An adult beetle emerges from this cocoon after four months and gnaws its way out of the tree.

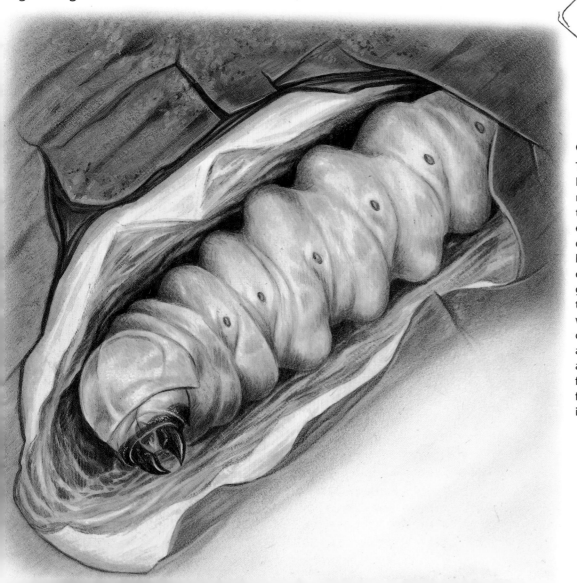

Did You Know?

● The harlequin beetle was once thought to be a type of grasshopper, partly because of its long legs and the peculiar creaking noise it makes when it walks.

● In the past, warriors of some South American tribes copied the beetle's elaborate patterning on their highly decorated shields.

● Because it looks so striking, the harlequin beetle is highly popular with collectors. It is easily caught by nicking the bark of a bagasse tree to make the milky sap, a favorite food of the beetle, flow out. The pungent sap attracts the beetle from afar.

● When threatened by an enemy, such as a bird or lizard, the beetle extends its long legs and holds them rigid. This, together with the short, sharp spines that dot its body, may make the predator think twice about trying to swallow it. The beetle also has jaws like gardening shears, which it can use to defend itself by giving nasty nips.

ASIAN LONGHORN BEETLE

Latin name: *Anolophora glabripennis*

WINGS

The transparent wings are normally folded up neatly under the hard, patterned wingcases.

LEGS

Like other insects, the beetle has six segmented legs. The legs of most beetles have tiny hairs that sense vibrations.

MOUTHPARTS

The jaws need to be powerful to chew their way through the tough bark and wood of tree trunks.

FEET

Each leg ends in a plate-shaped foot. Tiny claws are used for gripping any surface.

Beautiful but destructive, the Asian longhorn spends most of its life as a grub, chewing long tunnels in healthy young trees. It continues to attack the same tree until it weakens and dies.

This greedy tree muncher has even managed to hitchhike across oceans to continue its trail of destruction. Hidden in crates of goods shipped in from Asia, groups of beetle grubs have evaded U.S. customs and colonized a new continent.

The beetle grubs live unseen in the bark of wooden crates unloaded from ships. Inspectors spray each crate with chemicals, but often the infested bark is hidden on the inside of the crate.

1

Having escaped the poisonous spray, the grubs continue feeding. Later they turn into adults and chew their way out of the crates. They leave tell-tale holes in the wood and fine sawdust on the floor.

2

The adults fly off in search of a new home. Soon they will lay eggs in nearby trees. If a tree becomes infected, its days are numbered.

3

HOW BIG IS IT?

Actual Size

BUG FACTS

Length	1/2–1 in
Antennas	2 in
Diet	Living tree tissue
Range	Adult flies up to 1 mile
Lifespan	Grub 1–3 years; adult up to 2 years

The beetle is native to Japan, Korea, and China. It became a major pest in the 1970s when it attacked huge plantations of poplar trees in China. It has since been accidentally introduced to the USA.

Did You Know?

● In late summer and early fall, when adult Asian longhorn beetles are most numerous, children in some parts of China are given sticks and sent into poplar groves to kill the swarming beetles.

● A tree can be swabbed with bleach to kill beetle eggs that have been laid in the bark. However, it is not a totally effective method of controlling the pest.

● U.S. customs inspectors believe that they catch less than 20 percent of the Asian longhorn beetle grubs entering the country.

● In China, the Asian longhorn beetle is called the starry-sky beetle because of the "celestial" bright white markings that pepper its shiny, coal-black body.

● More than 2,000 trees in the Brooklyn area of New York have succumbed to the beetle and it may soon spread to Central Park.

SABER-TOOTH GROUND BEETLE
Latin name: *Anthia* species

SCALE PATCHES
Two yellow patches mimic the eyes of a larger creature, to scare off predators.

WINGCASES
With no wings to protect, the wingcases are fused together. This forms a tough, shiny shell.

LEGS
Long legs allow the beetle to run swiftly across the ground. This makes up in part for its inability to fly.

HEAD
A large head supports the powerful jaws. The bulging eyes are keen enough to detect the small movements.

ANTENNAS
The long, slender antennas detect prey by touch and scent.

MANDIBLES
The huge curved jaws are pointed at the tip, with sharp, inner edges.

The saber-tooth ground beetle is a ruthless predator of small ground-dwelling creatures, attacking and killing them with its deadly, saberlike jaws.

However, it is unable to fly and makes a tempting target as it scuttles across the forest floor in search of its next meal. So this little beetle is equipped with scary markings, like a big pair of eyes, to frighten off enemies. If that fails, it has another powerful defense at its disposal—a secret chemical weapon that can help it fend off enemies much larger and stronger than itself.

HOW BIG IS IT?

Actual Size

A striped grass mouse collects seeds, unaware that it is foraging close to a saber-tooth ground beetle. Because many mice eat insects, the beetle can take no chances.

1

2 The beetle points its rear end at the mouse and sprays fine jets of toxin in the creature's face, forcing the rodent to retreat.

BUG FACTS

LENGTH	1–2 in	The various species of saber-tooth ground beetles can be found throughout much of Africa. Some are more at home in tropical forests. Others eke out a living in the desert lands of the southwestern part of the continent, such as the Kalahari and Namib deserts. The beetle is active mainly at night, hiding by day.
PREY	Small invertebrates	
WEAPONS	Powerful jaws and a toxin containing formic acid, made and stored in glands situated behind the abdomen	
LIFESPAN	4–5 months	

Did You Know?

● In arid environments, such as deserts, the saber-tooth ground beetle burrows long and intricate underground gallery systems in loose, sandy soil, in which it stores its cylindrical, maggotlike larvae.

● The ground beetle family forms one of the largest of all families of beetle, with an estimated 24,000 species found throughout the world. As well as the spectacular tropical species, such as the various species of saber-tooth ground beetles, large and colorful ground beetles are common in temperate regions.

● The European ground beetle (*Calosoma sycophants*) is such a fierce and efficient predator that it has been deliberately introduced into the USA in order to control serious infestations of tussock moth caterpillars, which can devastate all sorts of trees and leafy crops. During the short few weeks of just one beetle's life, it is able to kill and eat as many as 400 caterpillars.

BOMBARDIER BEETLE

Latin name: *Brachinus crepitans*

SPRAY
The beetle spurts this out with such force that it travels several times the insect's body length.

MOUTHPARTS
Sharp, scissorlike jaws can slice up slugs, worms, and grubs.

LEGS
Long legs give a good speed when running.

EYES
Compound eyes give good all-around vision.

BODY
The body is slightly flattened so that the beetle can slip under stones and logs.

WINGCASES
All beetles have a pair of tough covers to protect their delicate wings.

Beetles are high on the menu for a whole host of predators, big and small, from snuffling badgers and foraging hedgehogs to hungry shrews and colonies of ants. However, the tiny bombardier beetle has found an impressive way to protect itself.

When it is under attack, the bombardier beetle sprays a burning liquid out of its rear end, straight into its enemy's face. Stung and surprised, the predator hesitates for just long enough for the beetle to scuttle away to safety. First observed in 1750, the explosive spray of the bombardier beetle had scientists baffled for 200 years. It was finally explained by a German chemist named Schildknecht. The way it works is pure rocket science.

HOW BIG IS IT?

x2

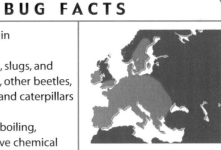

BUG FACTS

LENGTH	$1/4–1/2$ in
DIET	Worms, slugs, and insects, other beetles, grubs, and caterpillars
DEFENSE SYSTEM	Fires a boiling, corrosive chemical spray from its abdomen
TYPICAL USE	Usually a single burst, but can fire several, in rapid succession
LIFESPAN	A few weeks as an adult

The bombardier beetle is found throughout most of Europe, and is very common in some places. Related beetles with the same defense system occur in North America, including the popular *Brachinus frumans*.

1 Special cells (1) in the beetle's abdomen make two chemicals (*hydroquinone* and *hydrogen peroxide*). These pass into balloonlike storage sacs (2). Although mixed, the two chemicals form a harmless cocktail at this stage.

2 When the beetle is alarmed, the chemicals pass into the "blast chambers" (3). Here, glands release *peroxidase*, which acts like a detonator to trigger an explosion of spray out of nozzles (4) in the beetle's rear end.

3 In the explosion, the *hydroquinone* turns into *p-benzoquinone*, a corrosive. This generates so much heat that the water boils and blows the corrosive out with a loud "pop."

Did You Know?

● Charles Darwin, the famous nineteenth-century naturalist, once popped a bombardier beetle into his mouth for safekeeping while he tried to catch two other beetles. You can guess what happened next....

● Some beetles can use their defensive sprays to propel themselves across the surface of water like miniature speedboats.

● In one test, a bombardier beetle managed to fire 80 bursts of spray within the space of four minutes.

● In North America, a grasshopper mouse eats a bombardier beetle without being sprayed by jamming the insect's rear end in the ground.

VIOLET GROUND BEETLE

Latin name: *Carabus violaceus*

WINGCASES

The glossy wingcases shine purple in bright sunlight. Unlike most beetles, the violet ground beetle cannot fly.

EYES

Large bulging eyes let the beetle pinpoint prey at close range. But they are less effective in the dark.

ANTENNAS

Numerous touch and taste sensors on the antennas help the beetle locate its victims.

JAWS

Strong muscles power the ground beetle's shearing jaws, which easily pierce human flesh.

LEGS

Long, muscular legs help the beetle to move with surprising speed.

Prowling across the ground, jaws at the ready, the violet ground beetle is alert to the slightest rustle of movement or whiff of animal scent. This gleaming beetle is a merciless killer that pounces on its victims as they emerge from their homes or forage for food. It preys on succulent creepy-crawlies such as snails, slugs, and worms. Its powerful, pincer jaws soon make mincemeat of its prey.

HOW BIG IS IT?

Actual Size

BUG FACTS

LENGTH	3/4–1 in
PREY	Snails, slugs, worms, and small insects
WEAPONS	Powerful, shearing jaws
BREEDING	Female lays eggs in soil
LIFESPAN	Up to 2 years

The violet ground beetle ranges across most of Europe, through southern Russia to eastern Siberia and Japan. Although it prefers wooded terrain, it's a hardy species that copes with almost any altitude, and is common in urban areas.

1 A plump worm pokes its head out of its burrow. Quickly, the beetle scuttles over, clamps its serrated jaws around the worm and tugs.

2 The worm's long tail is still anchored firmly in the ground but the beetle hangs on tight. Suddenly, the beetle's jaws shear the worm in half, leaving the killer insect with a tasty, meaty meal.

Did You Know?

● Male ground beetles often fight if they run into each other during the mating season in spring, biting violently with their powerful jaws until one gives up and runs away.

● Although the violet ground beetle is basically a hunter, it isn't adverse to scavenging flesh from rotting corpses, and also nibbles at mushrooms and other fungi.

● The violet ground beetle is an impressive specimen. However, it has an even more imposing relative that grows to 2 1/3 inches long—the giant ground beetle.

● Tufts of sensitive bristles on the violet ground beetle's body help it find its way around in the dark.

● Violet ground beetles are a variety of carabus beetle. When threatened, many carabus beetles produce a musky substance from special pygidial glands, and if you pick up one of these beetles even for a short while, the smell can linger on your hands for hours.

TIGER BEETLE

Latin name: *Cicindela campestris*

WINGCASES _____

Glowing with metallic color,
the hard wingcases lift up to
reveal powerful wings.

ANTENNAS

These are covered
with touch and
scent sensors.

EYES

These are
large and
made up of
many optical
cells. This gives
a wide field of
view and high
sensitivity to
motion.

LEGS

Long and muscular,
the legs provide the
speed that make this
one of the deadliest
hunting insects.

JAWS

The jaws are equipped with
sharp "teeth" to carve the victim
into chewable chunks.

Strong, swift, and savage, this brightly colored beetle is built to hunt prey. The insect catches victims using speed and superior vision and then ruthlessly rips them apart. The green tiger beetle's bulging eyes enable it to see insect prey at long range before a victim can spot the deadly pursuer. However, this fantastic eyesight works only if the victim is moving. If the prey freezes, the beetle loses sight of its meal.

HOW BIG IS IT?

Actual Size

1 A busy ant is foraging for food, unaware that a green tiger beetle is close. Before the ant can run, the killer seizes the insect in its jaws.

2 The mighty jaws crunch through the ant with ease. As its victim struggles, the beetle begins to feast on the ant's soft insides.

BUG FACTS

LENGTH	Up to ¹/₂ in
PREY	Small mobile creatures such as ants, insect larvae, small spiders, and other beetles
WEAPONS	Big jaws, ferocious attack
LIFESPAN	Up to two years as a larva; a few months as an adult

Tiger beetles are found all over the world, but the green tiger beetle inhabits mainly sunny, dry heaths and flat, sandy terrain from the Arctic Circle to North Africa and right across Asia and Europe.

Did You Know?

● The name "tiger beetle" refers to the insect's predatory habits and stealthy hunting technique.

● Desert species have extra-long legs to stand high above the burning sand (a posture known as "stilting") and stay cool in the rising heat.

● Some species are so reliant on sunlight that the moment the sun disappears behind a cloud they stop moving until it emerges again.

● An Australian, nonflying tiger beetle species (*Cicindela hudsoni*) may be the fastest-running of all insects. One study calculates its top speed at about 8 feet per second.

● Some species of tiger beetles release an unpleasant musky or "fruity" smell from their anal glands in order to deter predators.

● Native Mexican tribes make an intoxicating drink by fermenting crushed tiger beetles in water.

NUT WEEVIL

Latin name: *Curculio* species

ANTENNAS

The antennas have a distinct "elbow" joint. This lets them be folded back when the beetle is at rest.

EYES

The weevil's eyesight is poor. It depends more on smell, taste, and sound.

ROSTRUM

This allows the weevil to drill through thick nut casings.

MANDIBLES

These tiny jaws at the tip chew vegetable material and drill into nuts.

FEET

The feet end in sharp-toothed claws for a firm grip on nuts and leaves.

BODY

The head and thorax (middle body section) almost merge into one.

Many a hazelnut, chestnut, and pecan has fallen prey to the drill-like snouts of these little beetles. To the nut weevil, a tasty, snug nut kernel is both food and an ideal nursery. Nut weevils look like cartoon beetles with their furry little bodies and outrageously long snouts, but they are superbly adapted for survival. Year after year, commercial nut farmers despair at the runaway success of these crop pests. Every region has its own pesky species, drilling holes and sowing their greedy grubs far and wide.

HOW BIG IS IT?

x2

BUG FACTS

LENGTH	Larva $3/5$ in; adult weevil $1/4$–$1/3$ in
ROSTRUM	Up to $1/3$ in
DIET	Larva: developing kernels of hazelnuts or acorns. Adult: fruit pulp, young hazelnuts, buds, leaf-shoots
EGGS	25–40
PUPATION	1–3 years after egg deposit
PREDATORS	Birds, wasps, flies, soldier beetles, small mammals
LIFESPAN	4–5 months as adult

Adult nut weevils live in woods, gardens, and orchards across Europe and in much of Asia. Hazelnut weevils occur in the USA east of the Rockies, and make a nuisance of themselves as far south as Florida.

A female hazelnut weevil is ready to lay her eggs. Using the jaws at the tip of her rostrum, she drills a hole in each nut. Then she turns and plants an egg in each of the holes.

1

Inside the hazelnut, the larva hatches after 8–10 days. It feeds on the growing kernel, growing bigger. When it is ready to turn into an adult, it will gnaw an exit hole.

2

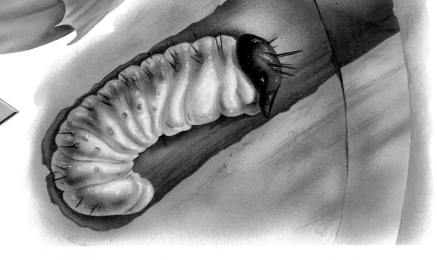

Did You Know?

● When alarmed, the nut weevil instantly enters a motionless state called *catalepsy*. Dropping to the ground and lying with its legs in the air, it pretends to be dead.

● Sometimes a female nut weevil loses her grip while drilling a nut and hangs from the trapped tip of her rostrum. If she can't regain a foothold, she eventually dies.

● Nut weevils have superb senses. They feel and taste with the aid of microscopic organs on the tips of their antennas, feet, and rostrum.

● In addition to nuts, adult nut weevils feed on the fruits of apple, cherry, peach, pear, and plum trees.

HERCULES BEETLE

Latin name: *Dynastes hercules*

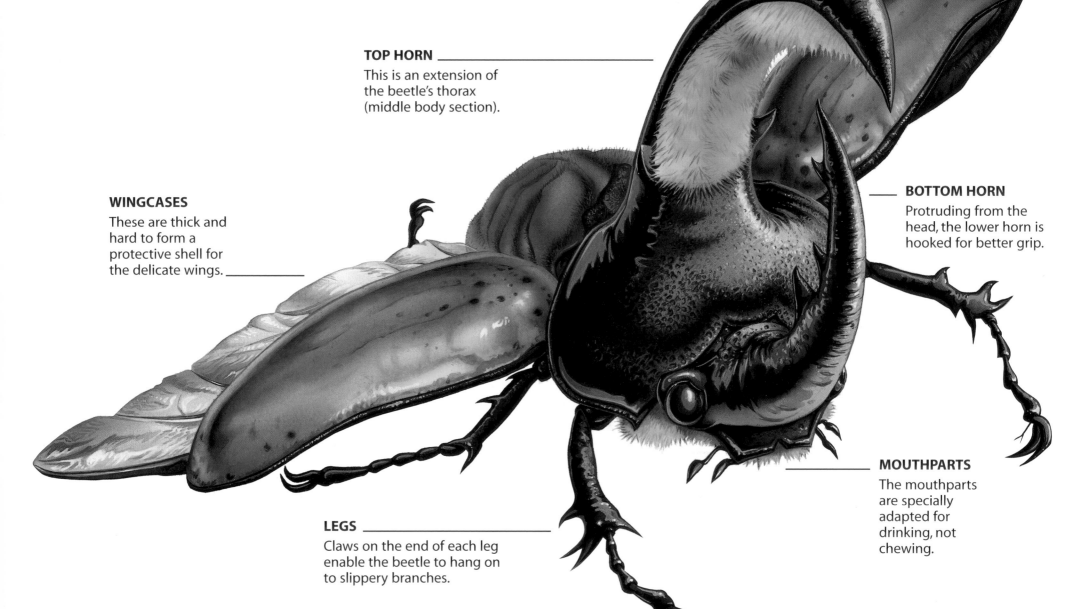

TOP HORN

This is an extension of
the beetle's thorax
(middle body section).

WINGCASES

These are thick and
hard to form a
protective shell for
the delicate wings.

BOTTOM HORN

Protruding from the
head, the lower horn is
hooked for better grip.

LEGS

Claws on the end of each leg
enable the beetle to hang on
to slippery branches.

MOUTHPARTS

The mouthparts
are specially
adapted for
drinking, not
chewing.

From the rear of the abdomen to the tip of the longest horn, this bulky rain forest dweller is as long as a man's hand. So a mighty male Hercules beetle more than lives up to his name when he locks horns with a rival in a titanic trial of strength.

The victor of the fight wins lush feeding and the pick of the females. On winning a head-to-head battle with a competitor, a male may carry off a female, holding her triumphantly aloft in his horns.

HOW BIG IS IT?

BUG FACTS

LENGTH	Male up to 7 in, including 3–3$\frac{1}{2}$-in horns; female up to 4 in (no horns)	The Hercules beetle lives in the trees and on the floor of the hot and humid tropical rain forests of Central and South America, where it ranges right across Amazonia. It is also found on some of the Caribbean islands off the coast of South America, including Dominica in the Lesser Antilles chain.
WEIGHT	$\frac{1}{2}$–1 oz	
DIET	Adult eats plant juices and ripe fruit; larva eats wood	
LIFESPAN	Unknown	

1

A male Hercules beetle lumbering along a branch finds another male blocking his path. The rival issues a loud challenge by rapidly rubbing his wingcases against his body. Furious, the first beetle charges, trying to knock his opponent off the branch. The rival stands his ground, and the beetles lock horns.

2

Finally, one of the Hercules beetles lifts the other beetle into the air and victoriously hurls him off the branch. Sometimes both beetles lose their footing and plunge to the forest floor. There they carry on the fight as if nothing had happened.

Did You Know?

● The Hercules beetle can change color to match its background or signal mood changes. In minutes, a yellow male can change to black and back to yellow. A thin, spongy layer on the wingcases shows yellow when its pores are filled with air. To make the dark color beneath the coating show through, the beetle squeezes water out through the pores.

● The larva of the Hercules beetle is a fat, pale grub that reaches a length of 5 inches and a weight of 1$\frac{3}{4}$ ounces. It lives in tree stumps and logs, where it munches its way through rotting wood for up to two years.

● According to folk legend in parts of South America, eating or wearing Hercules beetles makes you stronger and cures you of ailments.

● The Hercules beetle has such a liking for fruit that it sometimes finds itself packed up in a crate, shipped or flown across the world, and stacked on the shelf of a store.

GREAT DIVING BEETLE

Latin name: *Dytiscus marginalis*

HIND LEGS

Bristles on the oarlike hind legs increase the pushing surface.

WINGCASES

These protect the wings like a suit of armor. The female has ten deep grooves along each wingcase, while the male has only two.

BUILD

The body is streamlined to slip easily through the water.

FORELEGS

The beetle uses these to cling to weeds and grasp prey.

JAWS

These slash into victims like a pair of garden shears.

A tremor on the surface, a glimpse of hairy legs, and a flash of glossy green warn that a great diving beetle is about.

This aggressive aquatic insect is a voracious carnivore and scavenger, both as an adult and as a larva. The developing larva may not look much like its parents, but it is just as deadly, readily attacking virtually any small creature that it can grasp in its vicious, sickle-shaped jaws.

HOW BIG IS IT?

Actual Size

In the shallow waters of a small stream, a great diving beetle larva clings to some wispy strands of weed. Eventually, a small minnow strays too close to the lurking predator. With a powerful flexing of its long body, the fearsome larva shoots out and sinks its sharp jaws into the creature's side.

1

2

The larva hauls the feebly struggling fish up to the surface. It injects digestive fluids into its body cavity. These gradually liquefy the soft innards, allowing the larva to suck out the predigested broth.

BUG FACTS

LENGTH	$2\frac{1}{4}$–$2\frac{3}{4}$ in as a larva; $1\frac{1}{5}$–$1\frac{2}{3}$ in as an adult beetle (female smaller than male)	
DIET	Aquatic insects, tadpoles, newts, small frogs, and fish, plus carrion	The great diving beetle is found over a vast range extending from Western Europe, across central and northern Asia to Japan. It lives in weedy, still and slow freshwaters, from stagnant ponds and ditches to clean rivers and reservoirs.
LIFESPAN	A few months as a larva; up to 3 years as an adult beetle	

Did You Know?

● Though a strong swimmer and an accomplished flier, the great diving beetle is rather clumsy on land. It drags itself slowly over the ground and is highly vulnerable unless it can reach nearby water or become airborne again.

● Great diving beetles in search of a new home usually fly under the cover of dark and can easily become confused by the glint of moonlight from greenhouses or wet roads, mistaking them for water.

● The great diving beetle isn't immune from underwater attack itself. The hefty insect makes a juicy target for big fish, waterbirds, and aquatic mammals such as otters.

● If handled, the great diving beetle can inflict a nasty nip.

● Before taking off, the great diving beetle may open and close its wings a few times to make sure they are in good working order.

CLICK BEETLE

Latin name: Family Elateridae

WINGCASES

Like most beetles, a click beetle has a pair of thin wings that are protected by tough wingcases.

SHELL

A tough shell covers the thorax for protection against predators.

EYES

The compound eyes give limited vision, but enough for a click beetle to go about its business.

The strange little click beetle seems unremarkable enough as it looks for food among grass and leaf litter. But if it comes under attack from predators, it soon reveals its hidden talents.

Its first tactic is to fall on its back and play dead. If that doesn't work, the beetle can catapult itself away with a loud click, using a clever energy storage system. As it hurtles through the air, it spins itself around to land on its feet, then scuttles off to safety.

HOW BIG IS IT?

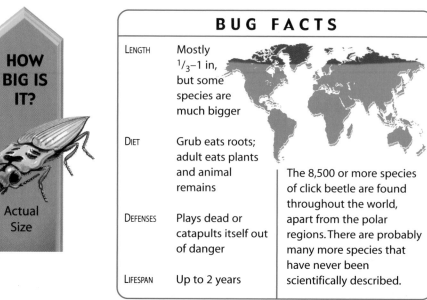

Actual Size

BUG FACTS

LENGTH	Mostly 1/3–1 in, but some species are much bigger
DIET	Grub eats roots; adult eats plants and animal remains
DEFENSES	Plays dead or catapults itself out of danger
LIFESPAN	Up to 2 years

The 8,500 or more species of click beetle are found throughout the world, apart from the polar regions. There are probably many more species that have never been scientifically described.

1 A coati finds a click beetle on a log and knocks it to the ground. It lands on its back and is unable to run away.

2 As the coati moves in to snap up the prize, the beetle activates its escape mechanism. With a loud click, it launches into the air, past the nose of its astonished enemy.

Did You Know?

● Some species of click beetle have luminous organs, like fireflies, and look similar to tiny rockets as they fly up into the trees at night. One newly discovered species even flashes green and red, almost like a miniature night-flying helicopter.

● Fossil remains of click beetles have been discovered in rocks that formed more than 140 million years ago, placing the fossilized insects at the end of the Jurassic period, when dinosaurs ruled Earth.

3 The click beetle somersaults through the air and lands feet first. It quickly scampers off to safety.

● African click beetles of the genus *Tetralobus* can grow as long as 2³/₄ inches, which is gigantic for a click beetle, and quite big by the standards of most insects.

SKUNK BEETLE

Latin name: *Eleodes longicollis*

WINGCASES

These hardened forewings are fused together to help conserve body moisture. This means the beetle can't fly away from danger.

HIND LEGS

Long hind legs enable the beetle to adopt its defensive headstand posture, but make it rather slow and ungainly.

ANTENNAS

These are loaded with chemical sensors. They probe the night air for the slightest scent of food.

SPRAY

The smelly spray is forced out of narrow nozzles at high speed. It travels several times the beetle's length. This lets the insect repel an attack before the enemy gets within biting range.

ABDOMEN

This contains the glands that produce its toxic chemical spray.

MANDIBLES

Sharp and strong, the scissor-action mouthparts shred fungus, excreta, and other such delicacies into a tasty pulp.

FEET

Small claws give good grip in dry, loose sand.

Desert life is tough, and a juicy beetle provides a protein-packed meal for many creatures. So, the slow-moving skunk beetle has evolved a highly effective way to keep itself off the menu.
At the slightest sign of trouble, the skunk beetle stops and thrusts its bottom into the air. Like a cannon pointing at the sky, it is then in prime position to fire a shot in the face of a prowling predator. Its spray of stinking gas stings the eyes, driving most enemies away.

HOW BIG IS IT?

Actual Size

BUG FACTS

LENGTH	$3/4$–$1^1/2$ in	The skunk beetle lives in the deserts and semideserts of New Mexico, California, Arizona, Nevada, Kansas, and Colorado in the southwestern USA, and in the same sort of terrain in Mexico. It hides away by day to avoid the heat of the sun, emerging at sunset to forage through the night.
DIET	Rotting plants and animals, fungus-ridden wood, and animal waste	
DEFENSES	Stinging, foul-smelling gas sprayed from its rear end	
LIFESPAN	3 years or more	

At sunset one evening, a hungry young coyote spies a plump beetle. It moves in for what looks like an easy meal.

1

Unfortunately for the coyote, this is no ordinary beetle. The skunk beetle squirts a dose of smelly gas at it. Nose and eyes stinging, the coyote runs away, yelping.

2

Did You Know?

● The skunk beetle is a member of the darkling beetle family, which has over 17,000 members, making it one of the largest in the world.

● The darkling beetle *Stenomorpha marginata* mimics the skunk beetle in appearance and posture, though it lacks its chemical defenses.

● Not all enemies are put off by the skunk beetle's chemical spray. Kestrels, owls, and plovers gobble up the beetle with relish, unaffected by its gases. The grasshopper mouse (*Onychanys torridus*) avoids being sprayed by pushing the beetle's rear end into the sand, where the gases discharge harmlessly. The mouse can then eat the beetle.

● Other beetles with a chemical weapon are the bombardier beetle (*Brachinus crepitans*), which lives in Europe, and its North American cousin *Brachinus frumans*. Both fire boiling, corrosive liquid out of an "explosion chamber" in the end of the abdomen.

GOLIATH BEETLE

Latin name: *Goliathus* species

WINGS

When not flying, the beetle folds its delicate hind wings neatly beneath the armored forewings. ———

COLORING

Each species has a distinctive mix of colors and patterns. As well as black and white, there may be coatings of yellow, fawn, brown, or rusty red.

LEGS

Each leg has a pair of claws to give the beast extra grip when climbing. This makes the beetle hard to dislodge.

ARMOR

The bulky body is encased in thick armor, which protects its soft body parts and wings.

HORN

Only the male possesses a horn. This is used in combat with rivals.

With a loud whir of wings and an audible smack, a big flying creature plonks itself onto a branch. Is it a bird? No, it's a goliath beetle. Growing as big as a mouse, the goliath beetle is a real giant of the insect world.

The goliath beetle gains its bulk during its larval (grub) stage. After hatching, the grub grows huge on a diet of plant matter. When it finally stops eating, its skin forms a tough shell. Inside this shell, the hefty grub is totally transformed.

HOW BIG IS IT?

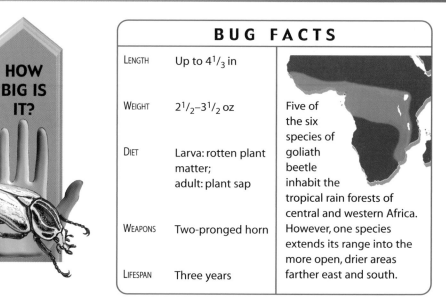

	BUG FACTS	
LENGTH	Up to 4⅓ in	
WEIGHT	2½–3½ oz	
DIET	Larva: rotten plant matter; adult: plant sap	Five of the six species of goliath beetle inhabit the tropical rain forests of central and western Africa. However, one species extends its range into the more open, drier areas farther east and south.
WEAPONS	Two-pronged horn	
LIFESPAN	Three years	

1 The larva's body tissues break down within the shell. Over many months, they reassemble into the form of a beetle. Eventually, the adult insect emerges.

2 After a brief rest, the newly emerged female makes her first flight. Although she needs food, she's also driven by the urge to breed.

3 The female drops down close to two males who are locked in battle with each other. Staying carefully out of the way of the gladiators, the female waits to mate with the winner.

Did You Know?

● The strength and gripping skills of the goliath beetle are so impressive that the insect is difficult to pry from its perch. One writer described the beetle clinging on so hard that it was as if both beetle and branch were "forged out of iron."

● Some other tropical beetles actually exceed the goliath beetle in total length, but few come close to its hefty weight. The bulky elephant beetle of Central America has a greatly extended horn that makes up one-quarter of its length. Another lengthy beetle, the giant longhorn of the Amazon, has a more slender build as well as thinner armor than the goliath beetle.

● The goliath beetle is not the only outsize creature that dwells in the African rain forests. The goliath frog, a 33-pound record-holder that is big enough to swallow rats, lives here. These rich habitats are also the home of giant butterflies and land snails, and foot-long millipedes.

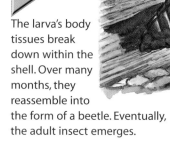

GREAT SILVER BEETLE

Latin name: *Hydrophilus* species

EYES
The large, rounded eyes provide a wide range of vision.

ANTENNAS
The short, hairy antennas collect air bubbles from the surface.

WINGCASES
The front wings have evolved into hard wingcases, which cover and protect the delicate rear wings.

BODY
The body is flattened and narrowed at the rear. The streamlined shape helps the beetle move through water.

SPIRACLES
These tiny openings absorb oxygen from a film of air.

The great silver beetle is a gentle creature. Poorly adapted to water life, it is a bad swimmer and mostly walks around on underwater plants. However, the larva of this plant-eater is a ruthless killer that can ambush and catch tadpoles and snails—and suck them dry.

The great silver beetle's voracious offspring will eat anything it can sink its huge jaws into. At first, the little killer feeds on microscopic organisms, but as it grows it tackles increasingly larger prey.

HOW BIG IS IT?

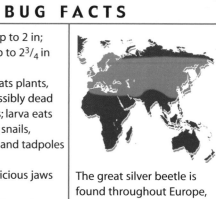

Actual Size

BUG FACTS

LENGTH	Adult up to 2 in; larva up to 2¾ in
DIET	Adult eats plants, and possibly dead animals; larva eats insects, snails, worms, and tadpoles
WEAPONS	Larva: vicious jaws
LIFE CYCLE	Female lays 50 to 100 eggs in a silk cocoon. These hatch after 11–17 days; larvae pupate after molting four times
LIFESPAN	Possibly 2–3 years

The great silver beetle is found throughout Europe, but is getting increasingly rare due to habitat loss. For example, it was once common in central and southern England, but now mainly inhabits a small area in the southwest.

Hanging from the water surface, a great silver beetle larva grabs a tadpole. The victim struggles, but the assassin plunges its jaws deeper into the creature's body.

1

2
The larva injects digestive fluid into the tadpole, dissolving the insides. The killer sucks out the soupy mixture, leaving behind an empty skin.

Did You Know?

● During the coldest months of the year, adult great silver beetles wait out the cold by hibernating in the mud at the edge of ponds.

● Adult great silver beetles use their wings to find mates or new places to live. They fly only at night, and often migrate long distances.

● During the mating season, the male great silver beetle calls to the female by rubbing the back edge of his wingcases against his abdomen to make a rasping sound.

● The beetle's larvae breathe via a pair of openings, called spiracles, at the end of the abdomen, which poke above the water surface.

COLORADO BEETLE

Latin name: *Leptinotarsa decemlineata*

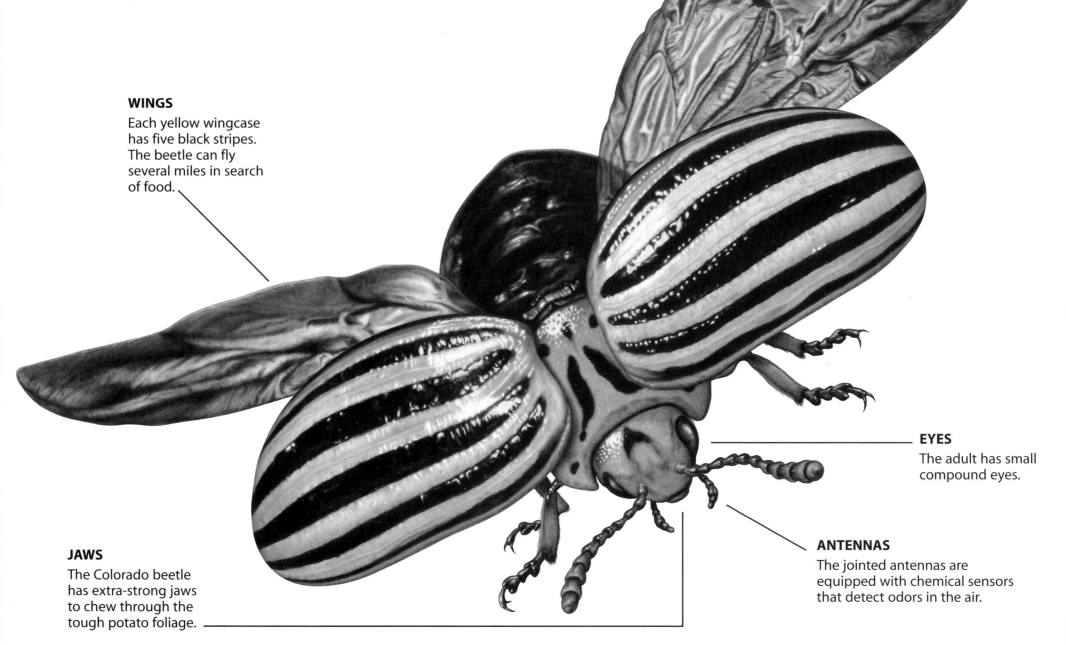

WINGS

Each yellow wingcase has five black stripes. The beetle can fly several miles in search of food.

JAWS

The Colorado beetle has extra-strong jaws to chew through the tough potato foliage.

EYES

The adult has small compound eyes.

ANTENNAS

The jointed antennas are equipped with chemical sensors that detect odors in the air.

hen farmers started growing potatoes in the mountains of the American west, they didn't know that the pretty, striped beetles eating the weeds nearby would destroy their crops, then multiply and spread like a plague across the world.

As the farmers soon found out, the Colorado beetle strips the foliage from any plant related to the potato. This includes deadly nightshade, despite the powerful toxins in its leaves. Once a female's eggs have hatched, her grubs continue the devastation.

HOW BIG IS IT?

x2

BUG FACTS

LENGTH	Larva $3/5$ in; adult up to $1/2$ in
EGGS	Lays up to 2,500, in batches of 20 to 80
DIET	Leaves of potatoes and related plants
LIFESPAN	1–2 years

First discovered in the Rocky Mountain state of Colorado in the U.S.A., the enterprising Colorado beetle has now spread to potato fields in Europe, Asia, and Africa.

1 After spending winter buried up to 20 inches deep in the soil, a female emerges in May. She settles on a deadly nightshade leaf and lays up to 30 tiny eggs.

2 Within 15 days, larvae (grubs) hatch and start feeding on the leaves. Without its leaves, the plant begins to starve.

3 Each larva sheds its skin three times as it grows. The final stage is a red, hump-backed blob that drops into the ground.

4 A week or two later, the larva has changed into an adult. The new adult may then produce a new generation.

Did You Know?

● The Colorado beetle became so famous when it first arrived in Europe in the 1870s that you could buy jewelry made in the shape of Colorado beetles, and even a box of chocolates with a picture of the beetles on the lid.

● If a Colorado beetle is seriously alarmed, it tries to escape attack by lying on its back, pretending to be dead.

● In winter, beetles hibernating underground may be killed when people sweep away snow, as this allows the frost to chill them.

● The Colorado beetle's only allies are antismoking campaigners. The beetle attacks the tobacco plant. Smoking tobacco kills three million people each year, causing 20 percent of deaths in the developed world.

● Measures to combat Colorado beetles include rotating crops and digging trenches around potato fields.

STAG BEETLE

Latin name: *Lucanus cervus*

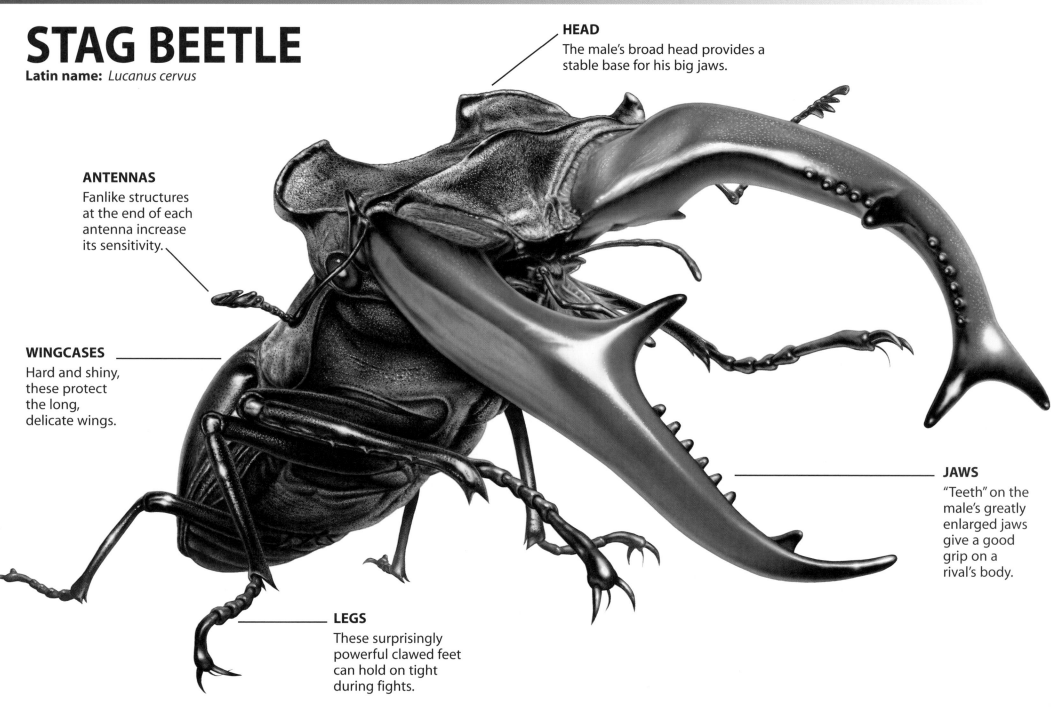

HEAD
The male's broad head provides a stable base for his big jaws.

ANTENNAS
Fanlike structures at the end of each antenna increase its sensitivity.

WINGCASES
Hard and shiny, these protect the long, delicate wings.

JAWS
"Teeth" on the male's greatly enlarged jaws give a good grip on a rival's body.

LEGS
These surprisingly powerful clawed feet can hold on tight during fights.

Brandishing a pair of mighty jaws, the male stag beetle is a fearsome-looking beast. In fact, he uses his huge jaws only to grapple with rival males, not bite enemies.

Male stag beetles may fight each other over the right to drink from a favorite source of tree sap, or they may fight for the right to mate with a female. Whatever the reason, the aim of the battle is simple: to knock the other beetle off its feet.

HOW BIG IS IT?

1 Sometimes, one male is so overawed by a rival that he runs away rather than fight. But not this time. Each of the heavyweights uses his jaws like a mechanical grab, trying to lift his rival, but not bite him.

2 At last, one makes a winning throw. Flipped onto his back, the loser may have real trouble turning himself over again. If he's really unlucky, he may lie there until he dies.

BUG FACTS		
LENGTH	Male 2–4 in, including jaws; female $^2/_3$–$1^1/_2$ in	
DIET	Larva (grub) eats rotting wood; adult beetle drinks tree sap	The stag beetle lives throughout central and southern Europe, from southern England and France in the west to western Russia in the east, and Italy, Greece, and Turkey in the south. Similar, related species occur all over the world.
LIFESPAN	3–5 years as a larva; 4–5 weeks as an adult	

Did You Know?

 ● Stag beetles sometimes drink tree sap that has partly turned to alcohol. They then stagger around drunkenly until the effects wear off.

● In towns at night, stag beetles emerge from parks and gardens and fly around streetlights.

● The stag beetle is becoming rare in many areas due to the loss of the old oak trees it relies on for food.

● Before fighting, rival male stag beetles may try to intimidate each other with a scratching sound made by rubbing their legs or wingcases.

● The Romans believed that the stag beetle brought them good luck. But many of their enemies in Europe blamed the beetle for starting fires with an ember carried in its jaws.

● The Japanese love to keep beetles as pets. In 1999, a Japanese businessman paid a record $90,000 for a single giant stag beetle.

SAWYER BEETLE

Latin name: *Macrodontia cervicornis*

WINGCASES

Hard wingcases lift up to reveal powerful wings, on which the creature escapes from danger.

COLORS _____

Vivid colors act as disruptive camouflage. It is hard to spot the beetle among the dappled shadows on the forest floor.

ANTENNAS

The antennas are long and covered with sensitive touch and scent sensors.

MANDIBLES

The long mandibles, or jaws, have serrated edges to aid grip.

CLAWS _____

Each foot has a pair of tiny claws that enable the beetle to grip the bark of trees in its rain forest habitat.

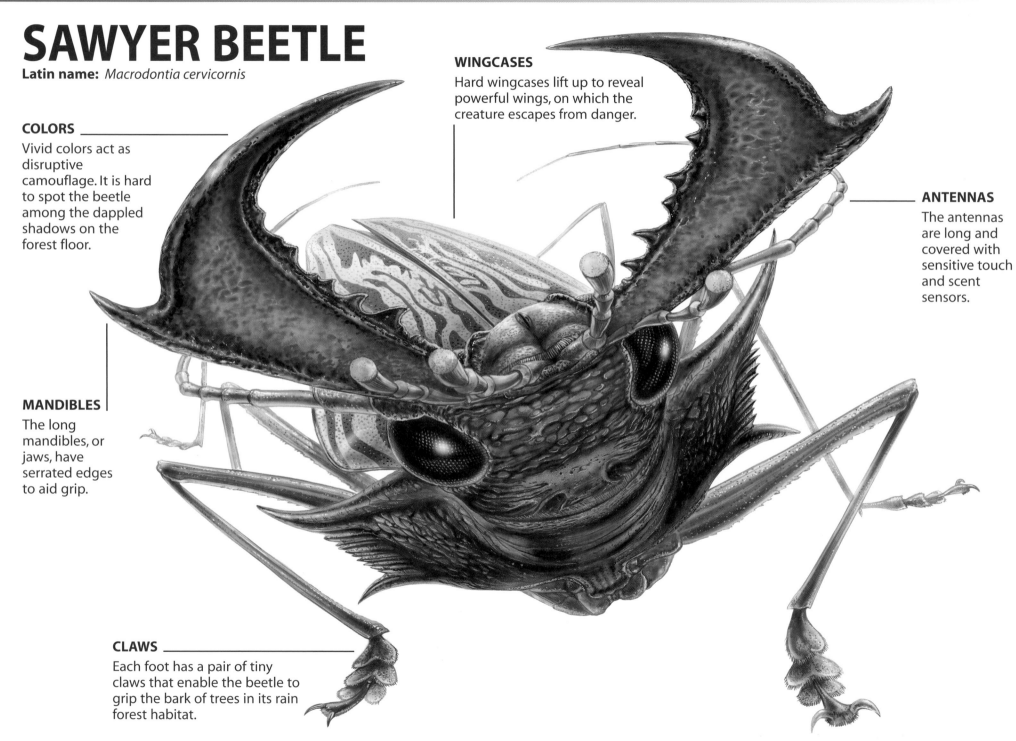

Deep in the forests of South America lurks one of the biggest insects in the world. With its huge serrated jaws and spiked armor, the sawyer beetle commands respect. However, the sawyer beetle isn't a hunter. It feeds on tree sap and rotten fruit, and mainly uses its weaponry for courtship battles.

This beetle, like other insects, has a different view of the world from ours. Its large, bulbous eyes are made up of thousands of tiny lenses, each showing a separate picture of the creature's surroundings.

HOW BIG IS IT?

BUG FACTS

SIZE	Larva: 10 in long; adult: over $6^1/_3$ in long, including 2-in jaws, with $6^2/_3$-in wingspan	The sawyer beetle is found in rain forests throughout much of tropical South America in an area extending from Venezuela and Colombia in the north to southwestern Brazil. Its larvae live exclusively inside the trunks and branches of fig trees, but the adults may be found on trees or among forest leaf litter.
DIET	Larva: the wood of fig trees; adult: tree sap, rotting fruit	
ENEMIES	Birds, mammals, spiders	
LIFESPAN	5–7 years, mostly as a larva	

1 The sawyer beetle's eyes are known as multifaceted, because they're made up of lots of separate panels. This means its eyes have limited ability to focus, but make good motion detectors.

2 If an enemy moves across the beetle's line of vision, each lens detects it separately and triggers a warning signal. The beetle is more sensitive to blue light than we are so the world looks different. Many objects reflect ultraviolet light. We can't see them, but the beetle can.

Did You Know?

● The aptly named titan beetle (*Titanus giganteus*), also from South America, has the longest body of any adult longhorn beetle with a length of just over 6 inches. Some sawyer beetles are actually longer than this gigantic insect, but the extra length is due mostly to the huge jaws.

● As well as being targeted by a wide range of predators, the sawyer beetle now faces a more serious new threat from us humans. Dedicated (and wealthy) beetle collectors are prepared to pay vast sums of money just for the dead body of an adult male sawyer beetle. Many of these insects sell for no less than $150 each, but the more spectacular examples may fetch even more, with one specimen reaching $18,000.

● Because of the growing trade in mounted specimens and the destruction of its rain forest habitat by excessive logging, this big insect is becoming endangered in some areas, including large parts of the Amazon basin.

ELEPHANT BEETLE

Latin name: *Megasoma elephas*

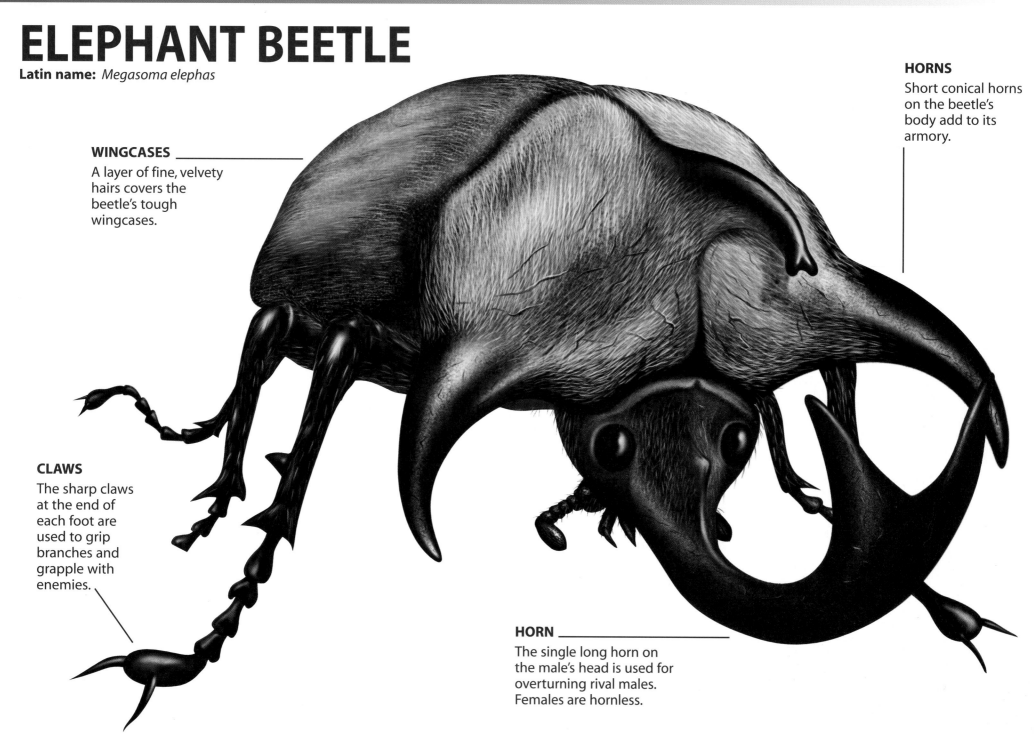

HORNS

Short conical horns on the beetle's body add to its armory.

WINGCASES

A layer of fine, velvety hairs covers the beetle's tough wingcases.

CLAWS

The sharp claws at the end of each foot are used to grip branches and grapple with enemies.

HORN

The single long horn on the male's head is used for overturning rival males. Females are hornless.

Clambering through the branches of his rain forest home, the male elephant beetle is like an armored warrior, ready to do battle with other males for territory or the attentions of a mate.

Whatever they are fighting for in the high forest canopy, elephant beetles are guaranteed to produce a ferocious gladiatorial contest whenever they meet. Like professional wrestlers, they develop cunning techniques for bringing their opponents down.

HOW BIG IS IT?

BUG FACTS

LENGTH	About 5 in	The elephant beetle inhabits the warm, moist terrain of lowland rain forests throughout the central isthmus of the American continent, from southern Mexico, south through Belize, Guatemala, Honduras, Nicaragua, Costa Rica, and Panama, to the northern forests of Colombia and Venezuela.
WEIGHT	Up to 1¼ oz	
WINGSPAN	About 9 in	
DIET	Grub: rotting wood; adult: sap and nectar	
LIFESPAN	4–5 years	

1 A lichen-covered branch is a main road for an elephant beetle. When two males meet, neither gives way. Horns raised, they prepare for battle.

2 After a long struggle, one of the beetles forces his horn under his opponent. He tips his rival off the branch. It's a long fall to the ground.

Did You Know?

● Beetle boffins have calculated that the elephant beetle is capable of lifting up objects up to 850 times its own weight.

● When flying, the elephant beetle's flapping wings create a loud noise that observers claim sounds just like a miniature helicopter.

● Sometimes, when big males are engrossed in a struggle for a mate, a smaller male sneaks past them and mates with the female while the combatants battle on unawares.

● Some forest tribespeople use the horns and other parts of the beetle as charms to give themselves strength and guard against disease.

● In North America and Europe, people pay enormous sums for dead elephant beetles mounted in frames as decorations.

● The elephant beetle is just one of 400,000 known beetle species.

BLISTER BEETLE

Latin name: Family Meloidae

WINGCASES

The wingcases contain a chemical called cantharidin. This poisons animals foolish enough to try to eat the beetle.

COLOR

Blister beetles vary in color from drab brown to vibrant yellow or metallic blue. The most colorful species often come from very dry areas.

LEGS

Each strong leg is tipped with a gripping claw.

HEMOLYMPH

When threatened, some blister beetles flex their knee joints and leak a chemical that cause blisters to the touch.

ANTENNAS

The threadlike antennas are covered in tiny touch-sensitive hairs and organs that help the beetle to detect scents.

Don't be tempted to touch this glossy little beetle. The briefest contact could leave you with blistered skin and a burning sensation similar to a nettle sting.

Many potential predators are put off by the beetle's bitter taste. If they do try to eat it, they risk death. The bodies of many blister beetles contain cantharidin, a strong toxin that causes internal and external blistering, sickness, and even death. A beetle outbreak can be a major threat to farm livestock—and horses in particular.

HOW BIG IS IT?

Actual Size

BUG FACTS

LENGTH	Female ¹/₅– 1¹/₂ in, according to species; the male is slightly smaller	Blister beetles are found in all temperate, subtropical, and tropical regions except New Zealand. There are more than 2,000 species altogether, and as they are most active in sunshine they are most widespread in warm, dry climates.
DIET	Larva eats insect eggs, and grubs; adult nibbles plants	
DEFENSES	Toxic secretions	
LIFESPAN	About 1 year	

A farmer puts his horse out to graze, not realizing that the pasture is infested with tiny blister beetles. The hungry animal is soon munching large mouthfuls of grass. It accidentally swallows a few of the beetles with its meal.

1

Before long, the unfortunate horse is gripped by terrible stomach cramps. By the time the farmer returns the next day, it has collapsed in the field and is close to death.

2

Did You Know?

● Some blister beetles are so full of energy from their long, food-rich larval stage that they don't eat at all during adulthood.

● Mother blister beetles abandon their eggs as soon as they lay them, but coat them with cantharidin to keep hungry egg-eaters away.

● When scientists first discovered blister beetle larvae, they called them "bee-lice," because they were clinging by their jaws to the leg-hairs of bees.

● On hatching, a blister beetle larva has unusually long legs, but these become shorter with every molt, until it looks like any other grub.

● Blister beetle larvae may survive only a few days unless a "host" insect takes them to a food source.

● Mating is a time-consuming business for blister beetles, taking anywhere from 4–20 hours—so they sometimes eat while joined together.

SEXTON BEETLE

Latin name: *Nicrophorus vespillo*

EYES
Like most adult insects, the beetle has complex compound eyes.

COLOR
Bold red, orange, or yellow markings warn predators that the beetle tastes horrible.

WINGCASES
The hind wings are protected by forewings that are modified into hard, strong wingcases.

LEGS
Strong, spiny legs make efficient diggers.

THORAX
The front section of the body is packed with strong flight muscles, so the beetle can search far and wide for a carcass.

ANTENNAS
The jointed, clubbed antennas have sensitive chemical receptors for detecting the scent of dead animals.

The smell of death is irresistible to the sexton beetle. When it sniffs out the fresh corpse of a small animal, it immediately sets to work burying it—complete with a batch of beetle eggs.

These resourceful beetles make superefficient use of a dead body. Not only do they store it as a supply of raw meat for their larvae as they grow, it also provides food for the female as she guards and cares for her young. The sexton beetle even carries around a team of mites that act as a cleanup squad for any fly eggs or maggots already in the corpse.

HOW BIG IS IT?

Actual Size

BUG FACTS

LENGTH	$5/8$ in
DIET	Dead animals
LIFESTYLE	Adults live in pairs
EGGS LAID	Up to 24
LIFESPAN	Up to 300 days

The sexton beetle, *Nicrophorus vespillo,* is found throughout Europe, Scandinavia, and much of northern Asia, as well as North America. Other species of sexton beetle live all over the world.

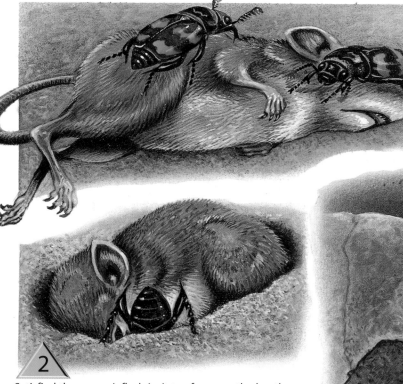

1 A pair of sexton beetles homes in on the smell of a dead mouse. They land on the corpse and check carefully to make sure it is still fresh.

2 Satisfied the mouse's flesh isn't too far gone, the beetles start digging a burial chamber beneath it. The corpse slumps into a ball as it sinks into its grave.

3 The beetles skin and dismember the corpse, then seal the tomb with soil. After laying her eggs in a side chamber, the female dines on the corpse.

Did You Know?

● The sexton beetle can smell a carcass from almost two miles away.

● Several pairs may land on a body, but after a fight the first pair to arrive usually fends off the others.

● If a male finds himself alone on a carcass, he attracts a female by releasing a special fragrance, called a pheromone, into the air.

● If the ground is hard beneath a corpse, the beetle drags it to a soft site. The insect is astonishingly strong. One pair can move a rat.

● The high-protein diet of young sexton beetles means they grow fast, doubling their weight in the first seven hours after hatching. This ensures they are ready to turn into adults before their food supply is too rotten to eat.

● When the female sexton beetle is caring for her brood, she "chirps" softly by rubbing her wingcases.

DUNG BEETLE

Latin name: *Scarabaeus sacer, Gymnopleurus virens, Phanacus bonnariensis,* and others

HEAD GEAR

Most dung beetles have flattened heads that they use like miniature shovels as they dig for dung. But the males of some species have big horns on their heads instead. They use these to fight over females.

FRONT LEGS

The legs are broad and spiny with spadelike feet. They are the perfect tools for shoveling dung.

JAWS

Powerful biting jaws help the beetle slice through tough fibers in the dung.

There's nothing this big, burly beetle likes better than wallowing in stinking muck, and it spends most of its life buried in steaming heaps of fresh animal droppings.

Dung is rarely in short supply, but it dries out fast, so a fresh pile usually attracts a crowd of hungry creatures. Eager to claim their portion of this delicious feast, the beetles often resort to heated fights or try to steal another beetle's dung balls.

HOW BIG IS IT?

Actual Size

BUG FACTS

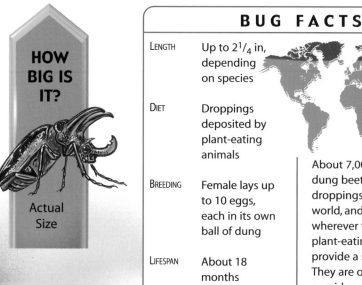

LENGTH	Up to 2 1/4 in, depending on species
DIET	Droppings deposited by plant-eating animals
BREEDING	Female lays up to 10 eggs, each in its own ball of dung
LIFESPAN	About 18 months

About 7,000 species of dung beetle collect droppings around the world, and they are found wherever there are enough plant-eating animals to provide a steady supply. They are only scarce in cold or arid regions.

1

After shaping a mass of droppings into a big ball, a dung beetle rolls its prize away. But as it trundles along, another beetle is attracted by the smell and flies down.

2

The dung beetles start to fight over the dung, wrestling with their front legs. Each tries to flip its rival over.

3

The invader proves too strong. With a mighty shove, it tips the first beetle off balance. It rolls the ball right over the unfortunate creature, embedding it in steaming dung.

Did You Know?

● In Africa, dung beetles are a favorite prey of the bat-eared fox, which uses its big ears to listen for them munching in their burrows.

● The ancient Egyptians used dung beetles as a symbol of their sun-god. They also believed that the beetles reincarnated, and gave them ritual burials along with their mummified dead.

● Native Australian dung beetles only eat dry kangaroo droppings, so when farmers started ranching, the sloppy cow dung mounted up and caused a plague of flies. Farmers solved the problem by importing other species.

ROVE BEETLE

Latin name: Family Staphylinidae

WINGS
Most species have two pairs. Small protective wings shield the delicate flying wings.

BODY
Long and narrow, the body is suited to a life crawling through narrow spaces.

JAWS
Strong and sharp, these make short work of unprotected insect larvae.

EYES
Large compound eyes help the rove beetle spot wriggling prey.

LEGS
Short but strong legs help the beetle to push its way through undergrowth.

Flesh and blood are favorites with most species of rove beetle. A keen sense of smell, a streamlined body, and big jaws make this tiny terror an extremely skilled predator. To increase its chances of successful feeding, it seeks out the best place to find juicy grubs, such as a rotting corpse or insect-attracting fungus.

Rove beetles also possess highly effective defenses to put off would-be attackers. These range from squirting an irritant liquid at an enemy to raising the tip of the abdomen and pretending to be a deadly scorpion.

HOW BIG IS IT?

Actual Size

BUG FACTS

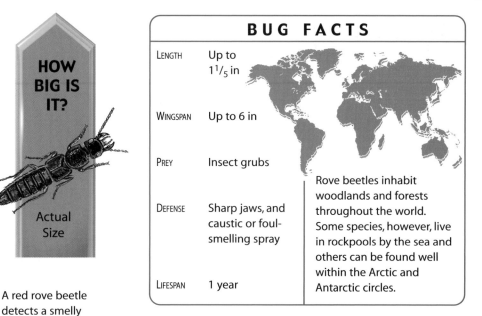

LENGTH	Up to 1$\frac{1}{5}$ in
WINGSPAN	Up to 6 in
PREY	Insect grubs
DEFENSE	Sharp jaws, and caustic or foul-smelling spray
LIFESPAN	1 year

Rove beetles inhabit woodlands and forests throughout the world. Some species, however, live in rockpools by the sea and others can be found well within the Arctic and Antarctic circles.

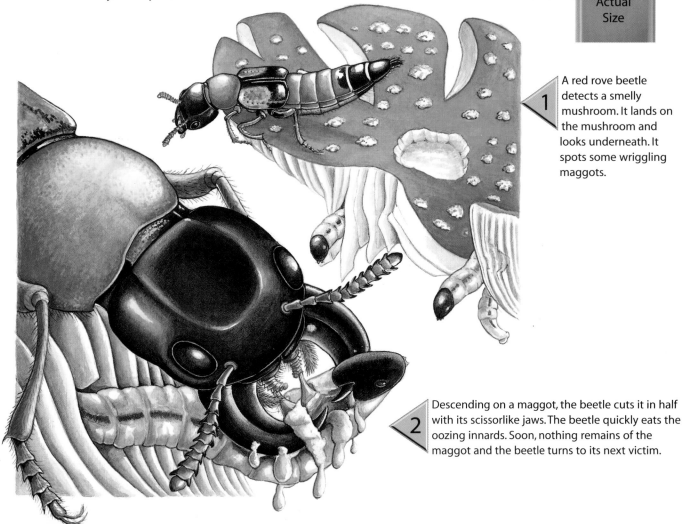

1 A red rove beetle detects a smelly mushroom. It lands on the mushroom and looks underneath. It spots some wriggling maggots.

2 Descending on a maggot, the beetle cuts it in half with its scissorlike jaws. The beetle quickly eats the oozing innards. Soon, nothing remains of the maggot and the beetle turns to its next victim.

Did You Know?

● One species of rove beetle surfs clear away from predators. The water-striding beetle squeezes a turpentine-like chemical from the tip of its abdomen. This spreads rapidly to form a thin film over the surface of the water. The force of this release pushes the lightweight beetle quickly away from danger.

● Some rove beetles are parasites. One species gets its bloody meal fresh from opossums, burrowing deep into the skin of the living host, and leaving only to lay eggs.

● A species of rove beetle called the devil's coach horse got its name after being frequently spotted in cemeteries. It also looks a bit like the black horses still sometimes used to take coffins to burial grounds.

● Some rove beetles that live with ants give off a chemical to stimulate brood-rearing behavior in the ants. The ants, in turn, feed the larvae of the rove beetle with regurgitated droplets of digested prey juice.

FOGSTAND BEETLE

Latin name: Family Tenebrionidae

MARKINGS

Fogstand beetles come in various colors. Some species are black, others have a white abdomen, and some are patterned with pale bands. White or pale markings help to reflect the heat of the desert sun.

JOINT

Hairs fringe the joints to keep out irritating grains of sand.

SHAPE

The head and thorax form a smooth wedge, helping the beetle burrow into the sand.

WINGCASES

The tough wingcases are fused, enclosing an air-filled space with breathing holes instead of wings. This reduces water loss through breathing.

LEGS

Long legs raise the beetle's body clear of the baking sand. They also let it push itself upright into the "fog-bathing" position.

MOUTHPARTS

Forked jaws nibble all kinds of plant and animal matter. Surrounding hairs gather moisture.

ANTENNAS

The segmented antennas (feelers) help the beetle find its way around.

Not many desert survival manuals would recommend standing on your head to collect water—but it has proved an effective survival strategy for the fogstand beetle.

Daily life in the desert is a nonstop battle for the fogstand beetle. Food and water are scarce and it spends its time dashing from one shady spot to the next, in constant danger of being baked alive. Yet it manages to survive in Africa's driest desert by using this clever method to collect vital moisture from the Atlantic Ocean air.

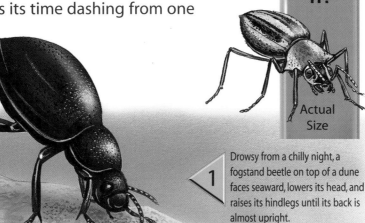

HOW BIG IS IT?

Actual Size

1 Drowsy from a chilly night, a fogstand beetle on top of a dune faces seaward, lowers its head, and raises its hindlegs until its back is almost upright.

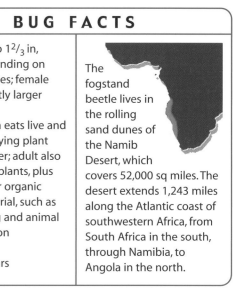

BUG FACTS

LENGTH	Up to $1^2/_3$ in, depending on species; female slightly larger	The fogstand beetle lives in the rolling sand dunes of the Namib Desert, which covers 52,000 sq miles. The desert extends 1,243 miles along the Atlantic coast of southwestern Africa, from South Africa in the south, through Namibia, to Angola in the north.
DIET	Larva eats live and decaying plant matter; adult also eats plants, plus other organic material, such as dung and animal carrion	
LIFESPAN	3 years	

2 The beetle stands as still as a statue as the early morning fog swirls in from the ocean. As the damp air touches its cool body, some of the water vapor condenses into tiny droplets. These roll down into its mouth.

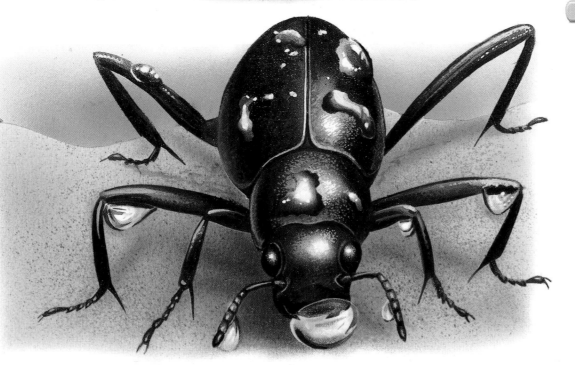

Did You Know?

● As long as the fogstand beetle has water to drink, it can survive for up to three years without food.

● Some species of fogstand beetles have ridges on their abdomen, which enable them to mound up tiny piles of sand to trap more moisture.

● Formed about 50 million years ago, the Namib Desert is probably the oldest desert in the world.

● In the language of the native Nama people of southwestern Africa, *namib* means "empty place."

● The fogstand beetle grub is one of the few insect larvae in the world that can absorb water vapor from the air. And it reduces moisture loss by passing almost dry feces.

● Found only in the Namib Desert, *Welwitschia mirabilis* is a primitive plant that obtains almost all of its moisture from condensed fog—just like the fogstand beetle.

GIRAFFE BEETLE

Latin name: *Trachelophorus giraffa*

HEAD JOINT

Hinged like a desk lamp, this allows the beetle to move its head up and down. Bobbing the head may help a male attract the attention of a female.

FEELERS

These are sensitive to smells as well as touch. The beetle uses them to sniff and feel around for food, mates, enemies, and rivals.

EYES

The beetle's small eyes are probably sensitive only to movement.

WINGCASES

When the beetle flies, the tough, protective wingcases flip open and the delicate, lacy wings unfold.

JAWS

The beetle has small but sharp jaws for snipping up leaves.

THORAX

The thorax (middle body part) contains the muscles that control the movement of the head.

CLAWS

Large, strong claws allow the beetle to grip tightly to leaves. In a breeze, it can hang on from any angle, even upsidedown.

Bobbing his oddly elongated head, the male of this aptly named insect looks more like a miniature mechanical toy than a living creature. Scientists know that the male giraffe beetle bobs his extraordinary head in this way to attract females to mate with, but they are still puzzled about why this method is so successful. One thing is for sure—the beetles could not breed in the way that it does if the female had such an extraordinarily long head, too.

HOW BIG IS IT?

Actual Size

The male giraffe beetle's long head is essential—and the longer the head, the better. The male must have evolved this peculiar feature over generation after generation.

1

When the female giraffe beetle lays an egg, she does so inside a leaf that she rolls up between her jaws and front legs. If she had a long head like the male, she would be unable to roll up the leaf tightly enough, if at all.

2

The maggotlike larva of the giraffe beetle lives in the safe confines of a rolled-up leaf. This conveniently doubles as an edible home. Like the adult, it has powerful jaws for chomping its food.

3

BUG FACTS

TOTAL LENGTH	Male $1/2$–$6/7$ in, almost half of which is the head; female $1/2$ in	
DIET	Both the larva and the adult eat the leaves of the large *Melastomataceae* family of tropical creepers and shrubs	Some 994 miles long and 280 miles wide, Madagascar is the world's fourth-largest island. The giraffe beetle is widespread in the northern and eastern coastal regions, in the island's rain forests, and other areas where creepers and shrubs grow. It became known to Western science in 1860.
LIFESPAN	Weeks or even months as a larva, then only a few weeks or even days as an adult	

Did You Know?

● Madagascar split from Africa 150 million or more years ago and for at least 40 million years has been too far away for life-forms to raft across. So most of the plants and animals on Madagascar have evolved separately from those in Africa and are unique to the island.

● The giraffe beetle's bright red wingcases may be a warning to birds and other predators that the insect is nasty to eat.

● Many species of weevil lay their eggs in rolled-up leaves, but not all bother to make their own rolls. Some, appropriately known as cuckoo weevils, lay their eggs in other weevils' leaf rolls.

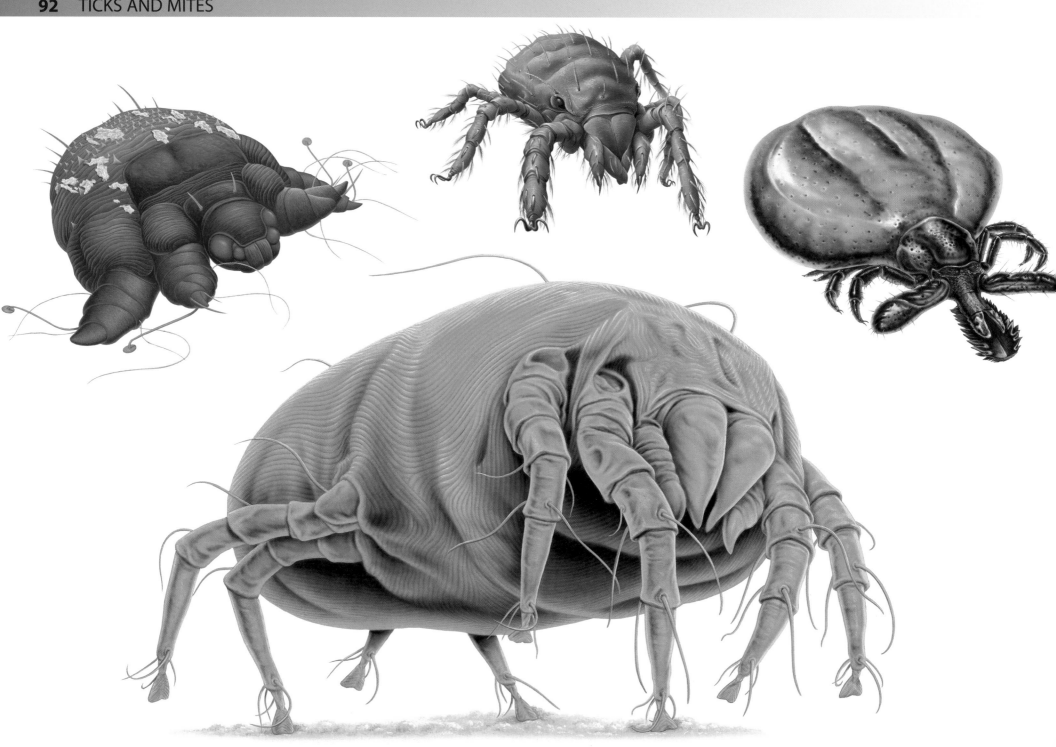

Ticks and Mites

Although not all of them look like it, ticks and mites are related to spiders. Many of them are parasites, which means that they live on other creatures and use them for food.

Ticks and mites belong to the arachnid order. This means that they have four pairs of legs, like spiders, not three pairs of legs like insects. But unlike most spiders, ticks and mites often live and feed on much bigger creatures, such as humans.

Ticks suck blood and carry diseases. They climb up the legs of animals and then attach themselves to the skin. They hold on tight with their mouthparts so they can't be knocked off. Once they have filled up with blood, the ticks drop off again. But they can sometimes leave lots of nasty germs behind them.

Like ticks, mites can also carry diseases. The itch mite, for instance, gets into the skin of humans and gives them a nasty skin disease called scabies. This causes itchy red spots on the skin. In animals, the same disease is called mange.

Other mites live in food, like flour or cheese. The dust mite lives in people's bedrooms. It particularly likes carpets made up of long strands of fiber. It has been said that a double bed can be home to as many as two million of them. There, they feed on the flakes that fall off human skin.

DUST MITE

Latin name: *Dermatophagoides* spp.

SETA

Hairlike seta are the dust mite's main sense organs. At the base of each setum is a single sensory cell that is stimulated whenever the setum touches anything.

SKIN

Patterned like a thumbprint, the skin is almost transparent. The internal organs give the mite its beige coloring.

PEDIPALPS

These cone-shaped "feelers" move bits of food to the mouth.

MOUTHPARTS

Food brought to the mouthparts is covered with saliva and then sucked in.

FEET

These give the mite a tight grip on the fabric.

LEGS

All adult dust mites have eight legs, like their cousins the spiders.

ust mites live everywhere, in countless hordes, wherever humans make their homes. They are too small to see, but dust mites are constantly creeping and multiplying all around us.

Feasting on tiny scraps of our discarded skin, they thrive in their millions, spreading their unhealthy waste behind them. They live among the fibers of our beds and carpets, where they can easily find the human skin cells that they eat. The dust mite's body is well designed to most effectively extract the nutrients from this food.

HOW BIG IS IT?

x125

BUG FACTS

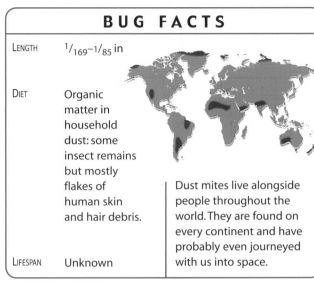

LENGTH	$^1/_{169}$–$^1/_{85}$ in
DIET	Organic matter in household dust: some insect remains but mostly flakes of human skin and hair debris.
LIFESPAN	Unknown

Dust mites live alongside people throughout the world. They are found on every continent and have probably even journeyed with us into space.

1 The dust mite does not have proper jaws to break up food particles. Instead, it soaks food with strong digestive juices. The juices turn the food into a soup, which the mite sucks up through its mouthparts (a).

2 In the mite's stomach (b) the food is absorbed through the stomach lining. Larger pieces of skin stay in the stomach until they dissolve further. Any excess food flows into the cecum (c). This "stomach extension" gets bigger the more the mite eats, causing the mite to swell up.

3 Waste material travels out of the stomach into the rectal sac (d). All the remaining water is then sucked out from the feces, leaving a tiny, dry pellet.

Did You Know?

● Human skin is shed in flakes, and the average person sheds about 40 pounds in a lifetime.

● Dust mites are more common in bedrooms than anywhere else. Their favorite habitat is the bed itself: an average double bed is home to about two million mites.

● Dust mites prefer long, loose-pile carpets to those with a short, tight pile. Long carpets gather more dust and moisture and offer the mite better protection against vacuum cleaners.

● Mites are among the oldest of land animals, with fossils dating back nearly 400 million years.

SCABIES MITE

Latin name: *Sarcoptes scabiei*

DORSAL SPINES AND SCALES
Angled backward, these mean that the female can move into the skin but not back out again.

LEGS
The mite uses its short, powerful legs to force its way along its burrow as it tunnels forward.

SETAE
Bristles radiating from the body detect chemicals.

CHELICERAE
These mouthparts are adapted to cut and slice into human skin.

PEDICELS
These stalks end in small suckerlike structures that help the mite cling to skin.

The scabies mite lives by tunneling into skin to feed or lay eggs. It may be tiny, but the mite can cause intense suffering. It is a parasite, almost invisible to the naked eye, which infests the skin of millions of people throughout the world, causing a disease called scabies.

A victim is usually blissfully unaware of the moment a scabies mite starts to burrow. Yet within a few weeks the awful itching begins—leading to sleepless nights and contant discomfort until a treatment is found.

HOW BIG IS IT?

x35

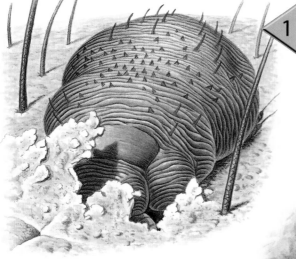

1 It takes about an hour for the female mite to burrow her way into the skin. Once under the surface, scales and spines on her back prevent her from going back out.

The female lives all her life just below the skin. She feeds on the fluid between the cells, which gives her the energy for egg-laying.
In a lifespan of two months, she produces up to three eggs a day.

2

BUG FACTS

LENGTH	Female $1/85$–$1/56$ in; male $1/127$–$1/102$ in
WIDTH	Female $1/110$–$1/60$ in; male $1/159$–$1/121$ in
HABITAT	Dry surface skin layers of human host
EGGS	1–3 per day
EGG TO ADULT	10–19 days
DIET	Skin cell fluid, dead skin, bacteria, fungal spores
LIFESPAN	Up to 60 days on humans

Occurs wherever there are human populations. Outbreaks of scabies are common in cool, humid, crowded conditions, particularly among people displaced by war or disaster.

Did You Know?

● Male scabies mites spend their whole lives wandering across the surface of their host's skin, looking for females and food.

● Males and immature mites offer a measure of compensation to their hosts by clearing hair follicles and the skin surface of harmful bacteria and fungal spores.

● Some scientists think there is a 15–20-year cycle of scabies outbreaks, governed by the growing and fading of the human immune response to the infection.

● Every year, there are an estimated 300 million cases of human scabies worldwide.

CHIGGER MITE

Latin name: *Trombicula* & *Eutrombicula* species

BODY

The head and body are joined together into one tiny, seedlike unit.

LEGS

Although an adult mite has eight legs, the chigger larva has only six.

CLAWS

Strong claws help the chigger crawl over its host and cling to its skin and hair.

SENSORS

Tiny, hairlike sensors on the mite's body help the creature feel its way around.

MOUTHPARTS

The chigger uses its sharp mouthparts to attach itself to skin and suck up its liquefied food.

Smaller than a speck of dust, chigger mites attack in droves, eating into your skin and driving you crazy with irritation and discomfort. Although not a bloodsucker, the chigger actually does something much worse. These tiny mites swarm onto your skin and squirt digestive juices that dissolve skin cells. As the mite feeds on the resulting liquid, the victim's body fights back by producing an itchy rash.

HOW BIG IS IT?

x125

BUG FACTS

LENGTH	Less than $1/102$ in	
DIET	Skin of many animals	
INFECTION	May carry organisms that cause disease	Chigger mites live all over the world, apart from polar regions, but are most common in damp, low-lying coastal areas with thick natural vegetation. The mite is particularly common in the tropics and subtropics.
VIRULENCE	Can be fatal	
LIFE CYCLE	About 50 days	

The chigger searches for a tender spot where it can feed. It finds the thin skin around a hair root. It slips its proboscis down the side of the hair root.

1

2

The mite feeds for only a few days. But the irritating rash produced by the mite's saliva can last for two weeks after the mite has left.

Did You Know?

● Although they attack humans, chiggers are not very well adapted to feeding on people. Most die soon after they start feeding, either because they get scratched off or because the skin's reaction prevents them from eating.

● Chiggers have been given many names by their human victims: red bugs, harvest mites, harvest lice, and harvest bugs are all chiggers.

● The chigger is often confused with the tropical chigoe, or jigger flea. This menace burrows into the skin of the foot, where it grows to the size of a pea. It then lays hundreds of eggs. If you think chiggers sound bad, jigger fleas are worse!

● There are about 20 known species of chigger mite, but there may be thousands more that have never been scientifically investigated.

● As well as humans, chiggers will attack birds, mammals, and reptiles.

HARD TICK

Latin name: Family Ixodidae

BODY ———————————

As the tick feeds, its body expands to make room for more and more blood.

SCUTUM ———————————

This hard plate shields the tick's small head and mouthparts.

LEGS

Each short leg has a pair of tiny claws for gripping.

HYPOSTOME ———————————

This feeding organ has more barbs than a box of fish hooks. Blood flows up a groove in its surface and into the tick's body.

CHELICERAE

This scissorlike organ cuts a neat feeding hole in a host's skin.

PALPS

These sense organs detect where the host's blood vessels are.

A tick is a tiny stomach on legs, with jagged mouthparts for sucking blood. When it feeds, it swells up like a blood-filled balloon. Forests and grasslands teem with ticks — relatives of spiders that feed only on fresh blood. Virtually blind and deaf, the hard tick must wait for a meal to be delivered to its doorstep. When ready to feed, it crawls to the top of a stem of grass, extends its legs, and waits for a passing meal.

HOW BIG IS IT?

x4

BUG FACTS

LENGTH	Typically $1/13$–$1/4$ in, but some species grow to $11/5$ in	
DIET	Fresh blood	There are several hundred species of hard tick found all over the world, wherever there are plenty of animals and people to keep them supplied with blood. They're most common in forested and grassy regions.
TYPICAL ATTACK	Prolonged but painless bite	
LIFESPAN	Up to 7 years	

An adult hard tick can survive for seven years without eating, but for every tick that feeds, many hundreds starve. This one is lucky. A passing man's bare leg brushes against it.

1

The tick settles among the hairs on the back of the leg. The tick slips its sharp mouthparts into his skin and starts to drink his blood. It feeds for several days until its body becomes swollen with blood. It then drops off.

2

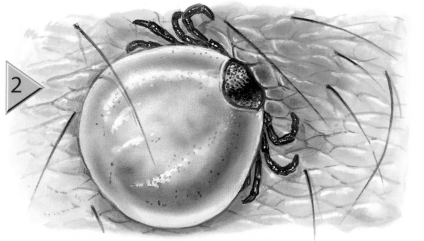

Did You Know?

● Scientists collect hard ticks for research by attaching a large square of cloth to the end of a pole and dragging it through tick-infested grass. The ticks attach themselves to the cloth, mistaking it for a host.

● The dangers of some tick bites weren't recognized until the 1930s, when Russian prisoners in Siberia began dying from a tick-borne brain disease called *encephalitis*.

● In some species of hard tick, the male doesn't feed from the host. Instead, he pierces the bloated body of the female while he mates with her and sucks up some of the blood that she has taken from the host.

● The hard tick hatches from the egg as a six-legged larva, acquiring its extra pair of legs only after molting into a nymph.

● As the hard tick feeds, the skin of its body doesn't just stretch to fill with blood, but actually grows.

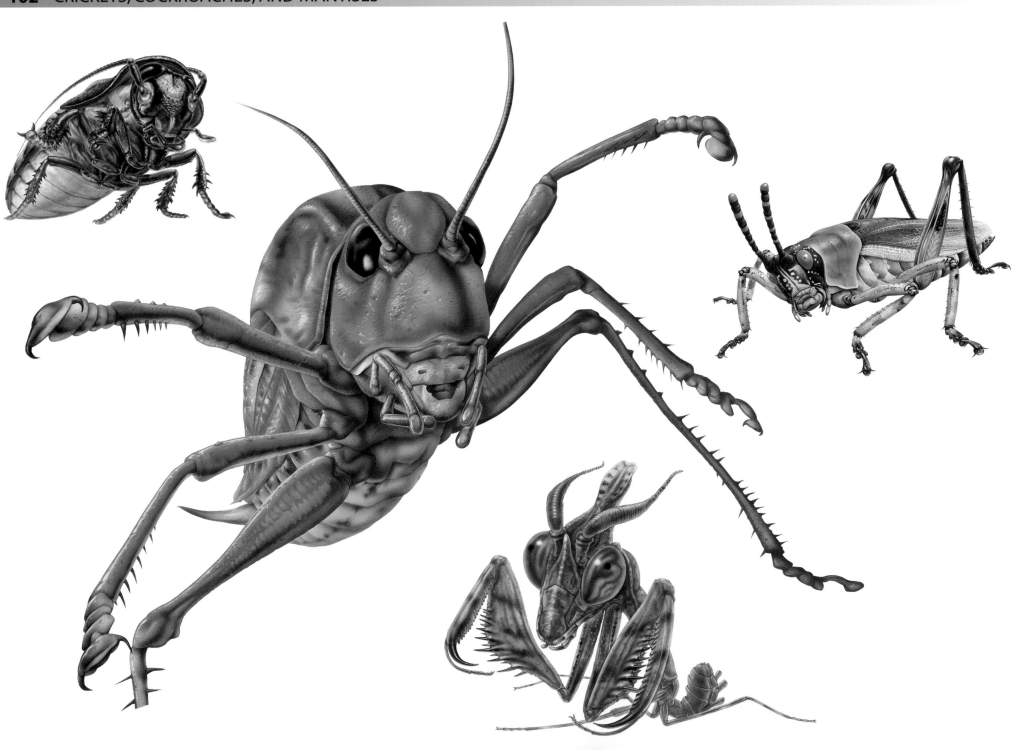

Crickets, Cockroaches, and Mantises

Although these insects are different, they all belong, or are closely related to, a group called Orthoptera. The name comes from Greek for "straight wing." There are around 12,500 orthopteroid species on Earth.

Crickets have flat bodies and pairs of long antennas on their heads. In the evening, in hot countries, male crickets make a chirping sound by rubbing their front wings together. Grasshoppers do the same. They are good at jumping long distances on their strong back legs.

Like crickets and grasshoppers, mantises and cockroaches are closely related. There are about 2000 species of mantis. Some types of mantis are called "praying mantises" because they hold up their front legs like someone at prayer. But mantises aren't religious—they hold their front legs like this to catch other insects to eat. Most of the 3500 species of cockroaches live in hot countries. Cockroaches eat almost anything and often spread disease.

Stick insects look like sticks or twigs as a disguise to stop other insects from eating them. They even protect their eggs by making them look like seeds.

WART-BITER CRICKET

Latin name: *Decticus verrucivorus*

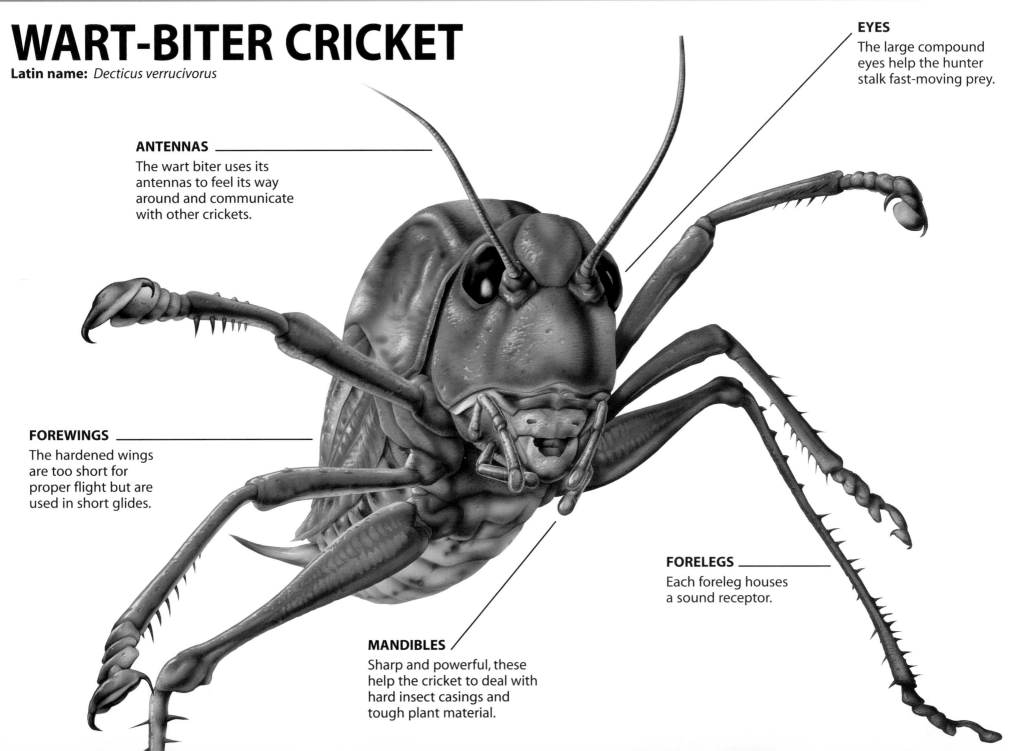

EYES
The large compound eyes help the hunter stalk fast-moving prey.

ANTENNAS
The wart biter uses its antennas to feel its way around and communicate with other crickets.

FOREWINGS
The hardened wings are too short for proper flight but are used in short glides.

FORELEGS
Each foreleg houses a sound receptor.

MANDIBLES
Sharp and powerful, these help the cricket to deal with hard insect casings and tough plant material.

This greedy insect just lives to feed. The wart-biter cricket eagerly devours all in its path. It will even chomp up snail shells, butterflies, and fellow wart-biters with its big, razor-sharp jaws.

The insect spends up to six years as a tiny egg but only a few months as an adult. With such a short time to grow in weight and find a mate, the wart- biter will munch anything it can find.

HOW BIG IS IT?

BUG FACTS

SIZE	Length up to $1^3/_4$ in; weight up to $^1/_{10}$ oz	
DIET	All forms of plant material; all types of invertebrate	The wart-biter cricket is common throughout most of Europe except the extreme south and north. It has become rare in parts of England, and numbers are also decreasing in Denmark and Sweden.
WEAPONS	Powerful jaws	
LIFESPAN	2–6 years as an egg; a few months as an adult	

1 A young couple finds a sunny spot to enjoy a picnic. But they're not the only ones to think about food: A hungry wart-biter cricket is gliding their way.

2 The cricket thinks the young woman's wiggling finger is a juicy pink grub. As the insect pounces, the hiker shrieks and lifts her hand. Startled, the cricket sinks its sharp jaws deep into her flesh.

Did You Know?

● It isn't enough that a female wart-biter hears the male's mating song: To locate a partner, she must also work out where the sound is coming from. The organ in the female's foreleg joint that she uses to detect sound has two slits that act as direction finders.

● The wart-biter cricket favors chalk grasslands and heathlands and requires a mixture of bare earth, where it lays its eggs, and tussocky growths of food plants, where it can hide from enemies, especially birds. However, changes in animal grazing patterns in the twentieth century have reduced viable wart-biter territories, especially in southern England and some other European regions.

● As a fully grown wart-biter can weigh up to $^1/_{10}$ ounce, it makes a nutritious snack for many birds. Live specimens that have escaped a predator's attack are regularly found lacking legs, and with peck marks on their abdomens.

GIANT WETA

Latin name: *Deinacrida* species

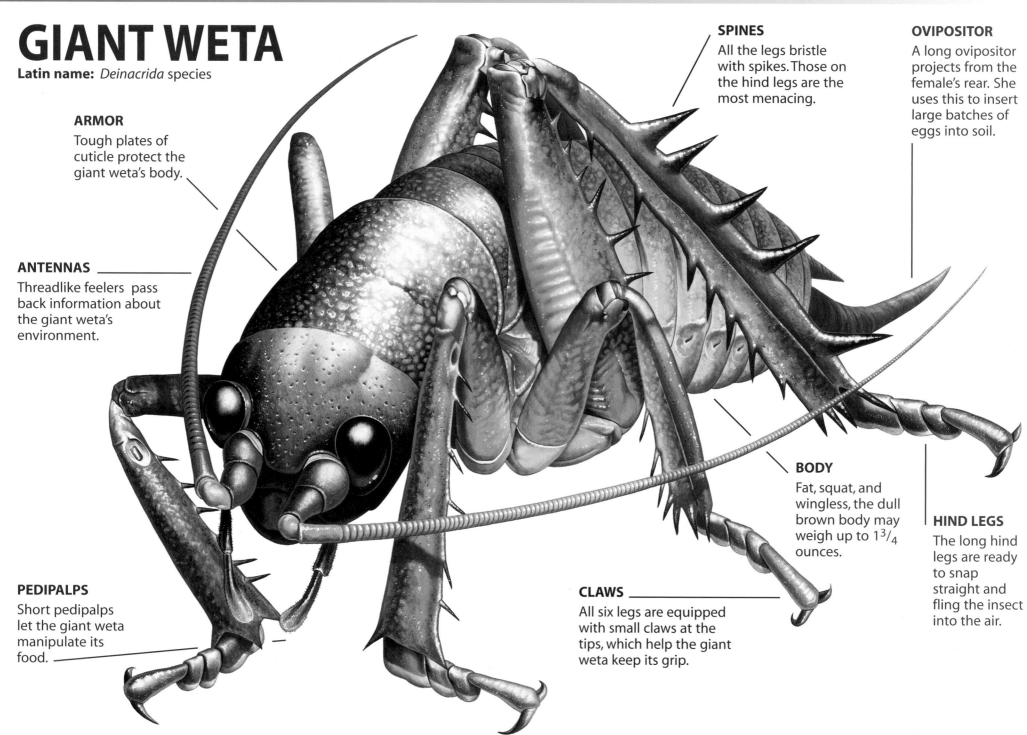

ARMOR

Tough plates of cuticle protect the giant weta's body.

ANTENNAS

Threadlike feelers pass back information about the giant weta's environment.

PEDIPALPS

Short pedipalps let the giant weta manipulate its food.

SPINES

All the legs bristle with spikes. Those on the hind legs are the most menacing.

OVIPOSITOR

A long ovipositor projects from the female's rear. She uses this to insert large batches of eggs into soil.

BODY

Fat, squat, and wingless, the dull brown body may weigh up to $1^3/_4$ ounces.

HIND LEGS

The long hind legs are ready to snap straight and fling the insect into the air.

CLAWS

All six legs are equipped with small claws at the tips, which help the giant weta keep its grip.

A giant weta is a monster of an insect: hamster-size with an armor-plated body and thick spiny legs. Its plump body makes it a target for predators, and it lacks the agility to rush away from danger. But enemies should beware if this lumbering insect holds its thorny hind limbs aloft. This signals that the weta is about to strike.

1 As dusk falls, a tuatara is out foraging among the leaf litter. It spots a giant weta emerging from a crevice. The fat insect looks like it would make a tasty meal, so the tuatara creeps closer.

HOW BIG IS IT?

2 Instinctively, the weta raises its spiked hind legs high above its body. The tuatara has fallen foul of these slashing spikes before. After a moment's hesitation, it decides to try elsewhere.

BUG FACTS

LENGTH	Female: up to 4 in	The giant weta was once common in New Zealand, for the only mammal predators were bats. But after Maori and other European settlers introduced animals such as dogs, the *kiore* (a type of rat), cats, brown and black rats, weasels, and stoats, its numbers fell dramatically. Today, its only refuges are Poor Knights Islands and Little Barrier Island off the northeastern coast.
WEIGHT	Female: usually up to 1³/₄ oz	
DIET	Leaves, ripe fruit, and dead insects	
DEFENSES	Spiked legs and strong jaws	
LIFESPAN	2–3 years	

Did You Know?

● Giant wetas take at least two years to reach maturity and end their lives in a flurry of reproductive activity. Once a male and female have paired up, they mate repeatedly over several days in the shelter of her lair. The male dies soon after, while the female survives just long enough to lay her final batch of eggs.

● The heaviest giant weta recorded was a 2¹/₂-ounce female. Over the next nine days, she laid hundreds of eggs with a total weight of almost 1 ounce.

● The only closely related species that still thrives on the mainland of New Zealand is the alpine scree weta, *Deinacrida connectens*, which lives on rocky mountain slopes at altitudes of more than 9,850 feet. It is extremely hardy, and is one of the few animals that can survive alongside glaciers.

● Giant wetas use the same hiding places many times, and a female may occupy the same nest all her life.

MOLE CRICKET

Latin name: *Gryllotalpa gryllotalpa*

ANTENNAS

These are shorter than those of most crickets so they are easier to use underground.

MOUTHPARTS

The mole cricket has powerful jaws for killing prey and biting through tough roots.

FORELEGS

These are the mole cricket's digging tools. They are large, spiky and extremely strong.

EYES

The eyes are quite small but still reasonably good. The cricket needs to be able to see when it flies.

HIND LEGS

These are short so the cricket can crawl down narrow tunnels.

Built like a miniature bulldozer, the mole cricket is perfectly equipped for a life spent digging in the soil. The male mole cricket also has very special skills. To attract a female to mate with, he digs an elaborate burrow shaped like a trumpet. It works like an echo chamber and is cleverly designed to make his "song" sound louder.

HOW BIG IS IT?

Actual Size

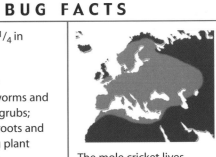

1 One evening in early summer, a male mole cricket selects a patch of soil. He starts burrowing with his broad, powerful forelegs. Then he backs out of the hole and begins again, digging another burrow.

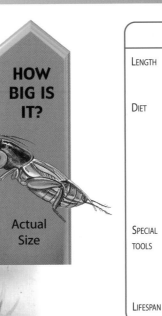

2 The two tunnels merge to form one bell-shaped burrow. The cricket compacts the soil to create a smooth-walled echo chamber. If he's done the job well, his courting call will soon draw in a female.

BUG FACTS

LENGTH	1 1/5–2 1/4 in
DIET	Mainly earthworms and insect grubs; some roots and rotting plant matter
SPECIAL TOOLS	Broad and powerful forelegs for burrowing
LIFESPAN	2–3 years

The mole cricket lives throughout most of Europe, Scandinavia, North Africa, and western Asia. It has also been introduced to the eastern USA. Some 60 related species are found around the world, on all continents.

Did You Know?

● Most crickets and grasshoppers have long, muscular hind legs for jumping away from danger. The mole cricket evolved from such a cricket but lost its long hind legs and ability to jump when it took to living in the ground. This doesn't stop it from trying, though: If attacked, it instinctively tries to leap into the air!

● The mole cricket may not be able to jump, but it flies well enough. On warm nights in southern Europe, swarms of mole crickets often buzz noisily around streetlights.

● The mole cricket is also a strong swimmer. If its burrow floods, it paddles its way out with powerful strokes of its broad forelegs.

● Grasshoppers and crickets broadcast their chirpings in all sorts of ways. Bladder grasshoppers (family Pneumoridae) have a nearly hollow, drumlike body. Tree-crickets (*Oecanthus* species) weave leaves with silk to make a soundbox.

ARMORED GROUND CRICKET

Latin name: Subfamily Hetrodinae

LEGS

An armored ground cricket uses its powerful back legs to kick at its enemies. The sharp spines can cause painful wounds.

FLUID GLANDS

Special glands release a nasty fluid to deter its predators.

CLAWS

The claws on its feet enable the armored ground cricket to climb and to grip plant stems.

ANTENNAS

These sensitive organs help the cricket to navigate at night. They are nearly twice as long as the body.

MANDIBLES

These are the insect's jaws. They chop through tough plants, dried flesh, and dead insects.

The armored ground cricket is built like a tank—virtually its entire body is encased in a series of spiky plates. It is a highly aggressive insect that deters much larger predators with its tough outer covering, disgusting taste, and vicious bite.

Hordes of these creatures scout the African savannah for food, eating anything they can find—even the bodies of their own kind. The hungry beasts can sometimes destroy a village's entire food crop.

HOW BIG IS IT?

BUG FACTS

LENGTH	Body 1²/₃–2¹/₄ in; antennas 4–4³/₄ in	Armored ground crickets are found throughout most parts of Africa. Only the sandy deserts are too inhospitable for them. The species that inhabit mainly southern Africa are known as "koringkriek," an Afrikaans word meaning "wheat cricket." In some years, plagues of the insects appear, posing a serious threat to cereal crops.
DIET	Plants and dead insects, including the carcasses of armored ground crickets	
EGGS	20–30, laid individually	
LIFESPAN	1 year	

Did You Know?

● Despite its name, the armored ground cricket doesn't spend all its time on the ground; it also looks for a bush or other low vegetation to climb up. It never tries to hide and is clearly visible to any enemies that may be passing.

● Native Africans avoid ground crickets, claiming they're poisonous. The species studied so far exude only a harmless, unpleasant-tasting fluid. But scientists haven't looked at every species, so there may be a "killer cricket" waiting to be found.

● Unlike many insects, the female armored ground cricket lays only a small number of eggs. Perhaps this is because its offspring are so tough that most survive to adulthood.

● The ground cricket's eggs won't hatch unless there has been rain in recent months. Without this, the soil dries like concrete, so the young can't reach the surface. The leathery eggs last for years below ground.

WASTE NOT WANT NOT
Thousands of armored bush crickets set out on a trek to find fresh pastures. Hordes of the insects swarm across a road. As some crickets are crushed by a passing car, others gather around the corpses, feasting greedily on their flesh.

PREDATORY BUSH CRICKET

Latin name: Subfamily Saginae

HIND LEGS

True crickets are agile jumpers. But this insect's spindly hind legs aren't built for hopping, so it walks instead.

WINGS

Predatory bush crickets don't fly and have weak wings or are completely wingless. Males have short forewings, which they rub together to make a "singing" sound.

COLOR

Most species of predatory bush cricket come in varying shades of pale green and brown, providing effective camouflage as they stalk their insect prey through the undergrowth.

OVIPOSITOR

This long, curved tube is used to deposit eggs in the soil.

JAWS

The sharp jaws deliver a crippling bite to prey. They can also give a painful nip to human fingers.

SPURS

Spurs on the edges of the legs sink into a victim's flesh and stop it from wriggling free.

Plant foods have no appeal for the predatory bush cricket. Relishing the living flesh of fellow insects, it tears into its victims with powerful jaws—and can give human fingers a nasty nip!

This sharp-eyed beast strides along on spindly legs, pacing slowly and silently in search of fresh food. Seizing its unfortunate prey in its spiked front legs, it gives its victim a swift bite to the back of the head and feasts hungrily on its innards.

HOW BIG IS IT?

BUG FACTS

LENGTH	Up to 4³/₄in, not including 1²/₃in *ovipositor* of females	
PREY	Insects, including other bush crickets	Saginae predatory bush crickets prefer warm, dry habitats, and are known from Europe (*Saga* species), Africa (*Clonia* species), and Australia (*Hemisaga* species). Other species of predatory bush cricket probably live in Asia, too, and there is a report from China that identifies a possible new species.
WEAPONS	Gripping legs with rows of spikes, and shearing jaws	
LIFESPAN	Up to 3 years	

1 A small predatory bush cricket is resting after a meal. It does not spot another, larger cricket creeping closer.

2 Shooting out its front legs, the big insect seizes hold of its relative. It holds the smaller insect tightly as it chews its head.

Did You Know?

● In France, the population of one species of predatory bush cricket, *Saga pelo*, seems to consist entirely of females. No males have ever been found, and the females reproduce without mating, laying batches of unfertilized eggs that are genetically identical to their mother—a process known as *parthenogenesis*.

● Predatory bush crickets bear many resemblances to an ancient group of insects whose fossilized remains date back to the Paleozoic era hundreds of millions of years ago—and are thought to be among the most primitive members of the Tettigoniidae, or bush-cricket, family.

● The predatory bush cricket's long, sensitive antennas are ideal for checking out potential mates.

● Cone-headed bush crickets can also inflict painful bites with their powerful jaws, even though these evolved for cracking open tough grass seeds rather than killing prey.

DESERT LOCUST

Latin name: *Schistocerca gregaria*

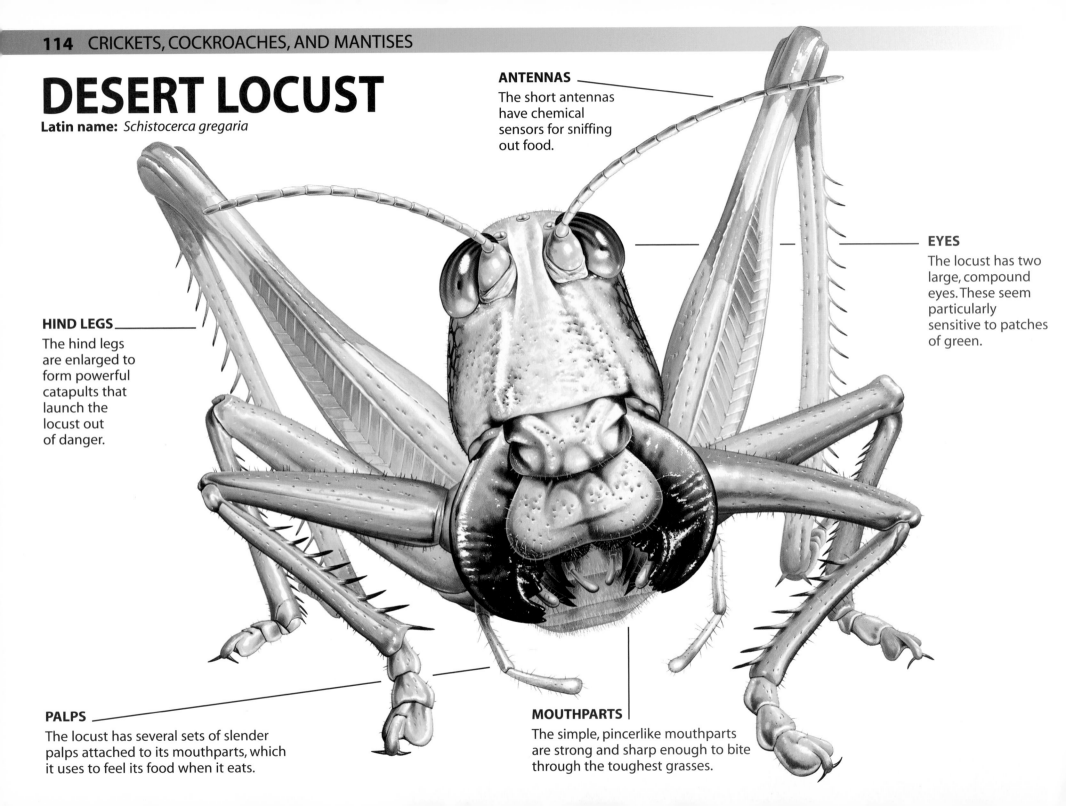

ANTENNAS
The short antennas have chemical sensors for sniffing out food.

EYES
The locust has two large, compound eyes. These seem particularly sensitive to patches of green.

HIND LEGS
The hind legs are enlarged to form powerful catapults that launch the locust out of danger.

PALPS
The locust has several sets of slender palps attached to its mouthparts, which it uses to feel its food when it eats.

MOUTHPARTS
The simple, pincerlike mouthparts are strong and sharp enough to bite through the toughest grasses.

Rainstorms bring a welcome flush of green to dry, dusty regions. But when the soil sprouts lush new foliage, desert locusts breed rapidly. They soon become an enormous, traveling swarm that spells disaster for any farmer it encounters. A gigantic swarm containing billions of locusts can blot out the sun, and the hungry nibbling insects will destroy any plant they come across.

HOW BIG IS IT?

DARK CLOUDS OF DESTRUCTION

A dense swarm of desert locusts descends on an African farmer's field, darkening the sky with the sheer mass of their bodies. The farmer watches in dismay as they strip the leaves from his precious crop of millet. He is powerless to stop the hungry hoard. In a few hours they will have devoured every last scrap of vegetation.

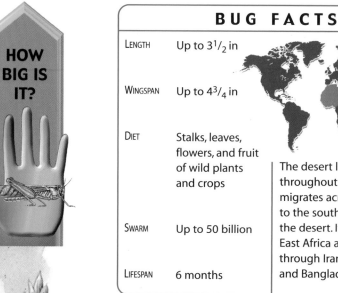

BUG FACTS	
LENGTH	Up to $3^1/_2$ in
WINGSPAN	Up to $4^3/_4$ in
DIET	Stalks, leaves, flowers, and fruit of wild plants and crops
SWARM	Up to 50 billion
LIFESPAN	6 months

The desert locust lives throughout North Africa, and migrates across the Sahara to the southern fringes of the desert. It is also found in East Africa and Arabia, and through Iran, Pakistan, India, and Bangladesh.

Did You Know?

● The desert locust has rows of tiny sensory hairs on its head, called setae, which it uses to detect air currents suitable for swarming.

● In 1961, a swarm of migratory locusts in southern Morocco ate 7,000 tons of oranges in five days.

● Swarms of locusts are often shadowed by flocks of birds such as storks and rose-colored starlings, which gorge themselves on the insects until they can hardly fly.

● To eradicate a swarm of 50 billion locusts, it would take more than 55 tons of insecticide.

● When locust swarms take off, their flightless young follow over the ground in a hopping, nibbling tide, until they too grow wings and join the swarm in the air.

● When locust swarms die, the few survivors lay eggs that hatch as ordinary, solitary grasshoppers.

ELEGANT GRASSHOPPER

Latin name: *Zonocerus elegans* & *Z. variegatus*

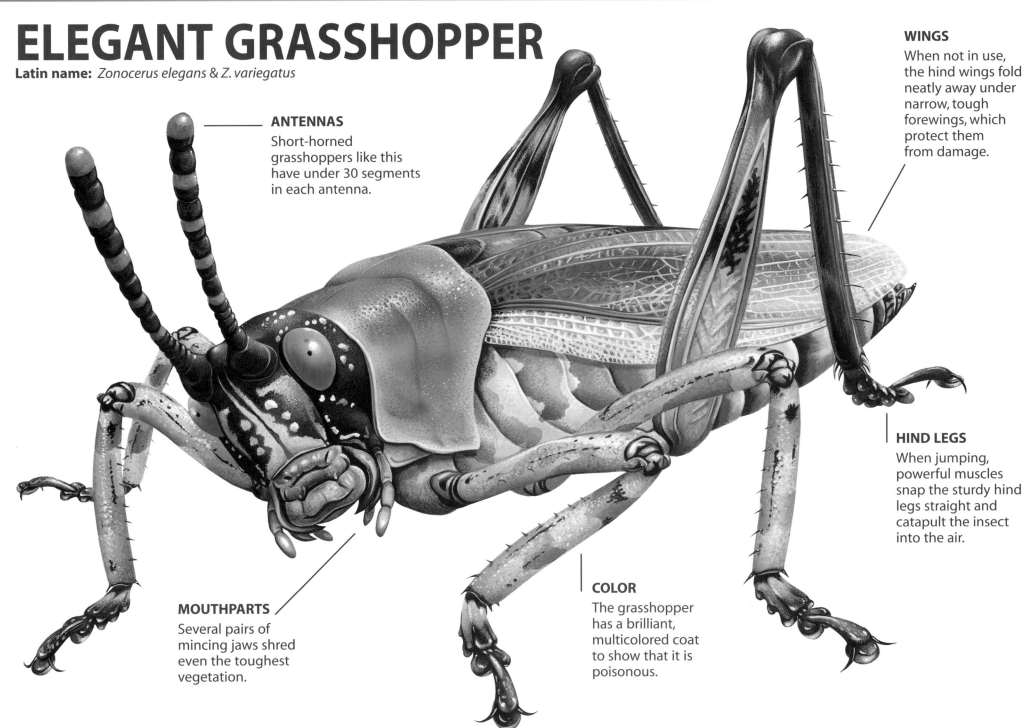

ANTENNAS
Short-horned grasshoppers like this have under 30 segments in each antenna.

WINGS
When not in use, the hind wings fold neatly away under narrow, tough forewings, which protect them from damage.

HIND LEGS
When jumping, powerful muscles snap the sturdy hind legs straight and catapult the insect into the air.

MOUTHPARTS
Several pairs of mincing jaws shred even the toughest vegetation.

COLOR
The grasshopper has a brilliant, multicolored coat to show that it is poisonous.

Grasshoppers are best known for athletic leaps and chirping calls, but this flashy African jumper has a much nastier surprise in store—it's poisonous. The elegant grasshopper gorges itself on toxic plants and stores the toxins in its body as a defense against hungry predators. Most enemies know they should leave them alone—and any predator unwise enough to try a bite will soon discover why.

HOW BIG IS IT?

Actual Size

BUG FACTS		
LENGTH	Up to 1⅓ in (female larger than male)	*Zonocerus elegans* is found from South Africa to Mozambique, Malawi, Zimbabwe, Zaire, and Angola, while *Zonocerus variegatus* is widespread in western and eastern Africa south of the Sahara. Both are equally happy in semidesert, dry forest, savannah, subtropical rain forest, farmland, or even gardens and they can be serious crop pests.
DIET	Leaves and flowers, including Siam weed, cotton, sweet potato, millet, and coffee	
DEFENSES	Stored plant toxins	
LIFESPAN	Less than 1 year	

1

A young jackal spots a colorful grasshopper in a bush. After a quick sniff, the inquisitive youngster gulps it down.

The poison soon gets to work. Running back to its mother, the youngster vomits up the contents of its stomach. It will think twice before eating one of these insects again.

2

Did You Know?

● Elegant grasshoppers usually reach pest status only in the dry season, and scientists think this trend may be linked to a lack of flowering Siam weed in the wet season.

● Few plant-eaters can stomach the bitter-tasting, toxic leaves and flowers of Siam weed—apart from the elegant grasshopper and some specialized insects and mites. It's also possible that these creatures use the ingested chemicals to send out signals about host-plant availability.

● Before jumping, a grasshopper jiggles its body from side to side so that the image of its landing spot moves across the lenses of its compound eyes. By comparing the various angles at which light strikes the lenses, the grasshopper can then calculate how far it needs to jump.

● Many big African grasshoppers deter potential predators by spewing a foul-smelling liquid from special glands near the base of their legs.

COCKROACH

Latin name: *Blatta, Blatella,* and *Periplaneta* species

THORAX

The middle part of the body is shaped like a wedge for pushing into tight gaps.

EYES

The insect has poor eyesight. Its eyes can tell light from dark, and detect movement, but little else. Being active at night and having good smell and touch, it doesn't need good vision.

MOUTH

Tough, toothed jaws allow the cockroach to tackle the hardest foods. Taste sensors can detect poison in food.

LEGS

The legs are long and muscular. The clawed feet can grip almost any surface, including ceilings.

ANTENNAS

These are covered with hairs that are sensitive to vibrations. They are also covered in pits that "taste" scents in the air, leading the insect to food.

The cockroach is a born survivor. A rapid breeder and wide-ranging scavenger, it defies most efforts to wipe it out with traps and poisons. Its tough body is equipped with sensitive hairs that alert it to the slightest danger. It can scuttle back into cracks and crannies with lightning speed if it is disturbed.

Few things are more revolting than the sight of a room crawling with cockroaches, and with good reason. Cockroaches spread filth and disease wherever they go.

HOW BIG IS IT?

Actual Size

BUG FACTS

LENGTH	$^1/_2$–$1^4/_5$ in, depending on species
DIET	Almost any organic, and even some inorganic, matter
DISEASES SPREAD	Include food poisoning, dysentery, cholera, and polio
LIFESPAN	Up to 2 years

Pest cockroach species are found worldwide, in warm, damp buildings wherever people live. They live aboard sea vessels and airplanes, and quickly establish new colonies when people move into new areas.

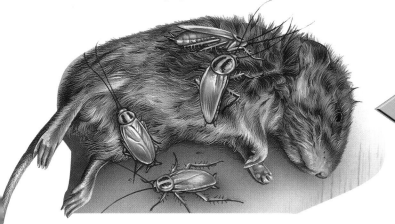

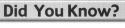
1 Under the cover of darkness, some German cockroaches home in on the corpse of a dead mouse. Nibbling at all parts of the decaying body, their legs, bodies, mouths, and guts are covered in harmful bacteria.

Did You Know?

 ● Fossil imprints of cockroaches in rocks show that they have lived on Earth in their present form for more than 300 million years.

● Cockroaches sometimes feed on fragments of food around sleeping people's mouths, even chewing eyelashes and eyebrows.

● Cockroaches were probably the first animals in space, as they are regularly found on spacecraft.

● One egg-case from a German cockroach could give rise to up to 7 million adults within a year.

● Cockroaches are remarkably resistant to radiation and would be among the few creatures on land to survive a nuclear holocaust—other likely survivors include rats.

2 Later that same night, some of the same cockroaches follow a scent trail to the back door of a restaurant kitchen. They squeeze their flat bodies through the slight gap under the door.

3 Within minutes, the cockroaches are scrambling over a plate of food. They hide when they hear someone coming. The waiter takes the food out to a waiting customer.

HISSING COCKROACH

Latin name: *Gromphadorhina portentosa*

ANTENNAS

The antennas have up to 130 segments, with receptors for motion, temperature, and scent.

BODY

The cockroach has a second "brain" near its tail. If its head is chopped off, it may carry on running around for several weeks until it dies of starvation.

MOUTH

Behind the mouthparts is a special chamber where food is mixed with saliva.

"EARS"

The cockroach senses sound with special receptors in its knee joints.

LEGS

The giant hissing cockroach has long legs to lift it up when it walks through leaf litter.

F ew creatures can surprise this giant cockroach as it forages by night. Its eyes have a special layer of reflecting crystals that alert it to the slightest glimmer of light. The ultrasensitive organs in its knee joints pick up even muted sounds. And it also has prongs on its tail covered with fine hairs that pick up the tiniest air movement.

However, if all this fails to keep the cockroach out of danger it also has an extremely noisy secret weapon.

As night falls, a hungry brown lemur spots a massive cockroach foraging on the forest floor. But as the lemur makes a grab, the big bug fights back.

1

The cockroach forces air out of two openings on its sides. The air comes out with such force that it "hisses" at a volume of nearly 90 decibels. Startled and deafened, the lemur drops its prey.

2

HOW BIG IS IT?

BUG FACTS

LENGTH	1–2$\frac{1}{2}$ in	
DIET	Fruit, fungi; other vegetable and animal scraps	The Madagascan giant hissing cockroach is one of two families of hissing cockroach found in the rain forests of Madagascar, an island off the southeast of Africa. Rain forest once covered most of the island's eastern coast, but today it is less than one-third of its original size as it succumbs to increasing pressure from farmers.
YOUNG	30–60 live nymphs	
MATURITY	7 months to 1 year	
LIFESPAN	2–5 years	

Did You Know?

 ● Native Madagascan people call the giant hissing cockroach the "kofokofoka," which sounds just like its hissing call, while early European settlers nicknamed it the "blower."

● The Madagascan giant hissing cockroach is one of the largest members of the cockroach family.

● In captivity, the giant hissing cockroach has been known to eat dog food, wallpaper, and whitewash, washed down with a sip of beer.

● Despite its reputation as a dirty insect, a cockroach frequently grooms itself. Taking its antennas in its forelegs, it pulls them toward its mouth and licks them, then carefully polishes its abdomen by stroking it with its spiny hind legs.

● Cockroach fossils date back to the Carboniferous period. These insects have been so successful in colonizing the planet, they have barely changed in millions of years.

ORNATE MANTIS

Latin name: *Empusa* species

ANTENNAS

These are longer in the male. Some species have comblike projections along both sides.

EYES

The eyes are poor at detecting stationary prey. However, they are able to spot fast-flying insects.

ABDOMEN

The abdomen contains a simple stomach. It's very flexible and can be curled right around over the body.

FRONT LEGS

Like a medieval instrument of torture, the spiked forelegs close to entrap struggling prey.

MOUTHPARTS

Powerful jaws mince food with side-to-side movements.

Even while hunting, an ornate mantis is a picture of calm tranquillity. But looks can be deceptive, as this gangling insect is always primed for a swift and deadly attack. With the sinister poise of an animal far more intelligent than a simple insect, the ornate mantis waits calmly to ambush its prey.

HOW BIG IS IT?

BUG FACTS

LENGTH	$^4/_5$–6 in
PREY	Insects, including other ornate mantises
WEAPONS	Camouflage, long, spiny forelegs, powerful jaws and lightning-fast reactions
LIFESPAN	Unknown

There are nearly 2,000 species of mantis, found worldwide in tropical, subtropical, and warm temperate regions. Ornate mantises are found across Africa, the Mediterranean region, and Asia as far east as India.

1

A young ornate mantis sits quietly on a flower. But she is not the only hungry ornate mantis in the area. A much larger male silently sidles closer.

2

Having moved into position, the larger mantis launches his attack. He shoots his spiny forelegs forward, trapping the smaller mantis in a tight grip. The male severs her head from her neck with his powerful jaws.

Did You Know?

● Almost a century ago, a respected French naturalist wrote that ornate mantis larvae were commonly kept as pets by invalids in hospitals "on account of their amusing antics." He stated that the mantises were fed on flies.

● A female mantis can turn her body in a complete circle to reach her abdomen with her mouthparts.

● The ornate mantis's genus name is *Empusa*. In Greek myth, Empusa was a demon with bronze feet that could change into a beautiful woman in order to seduce men.

● A mantis's pigment cells react to light. The insect becomes paler in bright light and darker at night. This improves the animal's camouflage and may help it retain body heat.

● In the southern United States, mantises are known as devil's coach-horses or mule-killers and are feared by superstitious people.

PRAYING MANTIS

Latin name: *Mantis religiosa*

FORELEGS

These are so fast that they can pluck prey out of the air in only a few hundredths of a second. The barbs grip and puncture the victim.

ANTENNAS

The "feelers" carry sensors to trace airborne scents.

HEAD AND NECK

The triangular head swivels on a flexible neck. This way, the mantis can keep both eyes on approaching prey without moving its body.

EYES

Large, widely spaced eyes give the praying mantis good binocular vision. It can judge distances very accurately.

JAWS

The jaws are sharp and strong enough to munch the tough bodies of insects.

Sinister-looking but cunningly disguised, the praying mantis waits to pounce on passing prey. Clutching a struggling victim in its outsize "arms," it goes to work with its jaws.

Keen eyesight and lightning speed make the praying mantis a highly effective predator. Once it has a victim in its spiky, clamping grasp, there is no escape. The best the luckless creature can hope for is a quick end.

HOW BIG IS IT?

Actual Size

BUG FACTS

LENGTH	Female up to 3 in; male up to 2¼ in	
PREY	Butterflies, grasshoppers, and other insects	The praying mantis is found all over southern Europe and in parts of northern Africa. It also lives in the northeastern USA, where it was introduced to control insect pests. Other mantises occur in all the warm regions of the world.
HUNTING STRATEGY	Ambush, catching its quarry with its spiny forelegs	
LIFESPAN	6–8 months	

1 Perched almost motionless, a praying mantis turns its head and watches as a fly buzzes close.

2 The unsuspecting fly comes within reach. The mantis shoots out its spiny forelegs faster than the human eye can see. It snatches the insect out of the air.

3 With a few bites to the neck it shears off the fly's head and settles down to its meal. It doesn't waste food, consuming every last juicy morsel.

Did You Know?

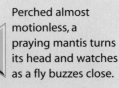

● The big mantises of the tropics eat small frogs, lizards, mice, and even birds, as well as insects.

● A mantis can only spot a moving target. If an insect keeps quite still, a mantis can walk right past it and not even know that it's there.

● In many species of mantis, only the male can fly. The female saves energy by not bothering, and lets prospective mates come to her.

● Nonflying mantises are deaf, but flying ones have a single ear tuned to the squeaks of bats, so they can hear a bat coming and evade capture.

● A mantis caught by one leg can escape by letting the limb break off. But if it loses a foreleg, it cannot catch prey and so starves to death.

● One species of mantis in the United States may be parthenogenetic, meaning it has only females, whose unfertilized eggs all hatch into more females.

FLORIDA WALKING STICK

Latin name: *Anisomorpha buprestoides*

THORAX
This body section has three segments for flexibility. Each segment bears one pair of legs.

SPRAY GLANDS
Just behind the head, these tiny organs make a strong chemical. Muscles around the glands squirt the liquid out.

COLOR
Glossy black and yellow stripes run the length of the long, slim body. This makes it look like a twig.

MOUTHPARTS
Small but powerful jaws snip pieces from the margins of leaves. More delicate jaws then chew the tough food to a pulp.

EYES
The small but bulbous compound eyes serve mainly to detect movement, especially that of a possible attacker.

LEGS
Tiny claws on the end of each long leg secure the stick to a swaying leaf or branch.

The Florida walking stick is so well disguised that birds searching for an insect snack usually don't notice it. But if the insect senses a predator is about to attack, it launches a first strike. If you're ever unlucky enough to disturb a Florida walking stick and it sprays you in the eyes, the pain is instant and excruciating. The agony eases after a few hours, but your eyes remain swollen and sensitive for several days.

HOW BIG IS IT?

Actual Size

BLAST OFF!

A Florida scrub jay spies a Florida walking stick near the end of a branch, and moves in for the kill. But the insect blasts it in the face with a dose of irritating spray—saving itself from being eaten.

BUG FACTS

LENGTH	Female 2–3$\frac{1}{6}$ in male 1$\frac{1}{5}$–1$\frac{3}{4}$ in
DIET	Mainly oak leaves, eaten at night
WEAPONS	A pair of glands containing a mix of chemicals, sprayed at an attacker
TYPICAL ATTACK	Both "barrels" fire at once in a sudden short burst
LIFESPAN	Months in the wild; longer in captivity

The Florida walking stick lives around the Gulf of Mexico, from Florida and Georgia to Texas, south through eastern Mexico to Guatemala and Belize. It is most commonly found in the outer branches of oak bushes and trees.

Did You Know?

● In the United States, many farmers once believed that stick insects poisoned livestock if swallowed. So they gave the insects such names as devil's darning needles, prairie alligators, musk mares, witch's horses, and (confusingly) scorpions.

● If a stick insect's leg is grabbed, it drops off, allowing the insect to escape. A nymph (young insect) can grow a new leg, but not so an adult.

● In some stick insect species, no males have been found. Females seem to hatch from unfertilized eggs; this is called parthenogenesis.

● Stick insects in captivity will sometimes nibble each other's legs.

MACLEAY'S SPECTER

Latin name: *Extatosoma* species

LEGS

The insect can snap off a leg in order to escape the clutches of a predator.

BODY

The insect's length, color, and spines make it look like a bunch of twigs and leaves.

CLAWS

The claws help the insect to keep a firm grip on plants as it moves.

ANTENNAS

These detect vibration and touch, and scent released by a mate.

MOUTHPARTS

The powerful chewing mouthparts make short work of tough eucalytus leaves.

This species has a clever way of keeping its eggs out of danger. The eggs look like plant seeds, with a knob of nutrients that ants can't resist. When the eggs drop to the ground, ants often take them back to their nest and snap off the knob to feed their young. They then put the egg in the nest's "rubbish" section, where birds can't get at it.

The tiny stick insect that emerges looks like an ant. It rushes around until it finds a way out of the nest, and climbs up into its host plant to start feeding.

HOW BIG IS IT?

BUG FACTS

LENGTH	Female 4³⁄₄ in; male 3¹⁄₂ in	
WEIGHT	Female up to 1 oz	
DIET	Eucalyptus leaves; also rose, pyracantha, hawthorn, oak, and bramble in captivity	
LIFESPAN	Female 1–2 years; male 1 year	

Macleay's specter is found only in Australia and New Guinea, where it lives mainly in densely forested areas. Altogether, some 2,700 species of stick insect are known to exist worldwide, mainly in lush tropical and subtropical regions.

A female Macleay's specter climbs along a branch. Hanging upside down, she flicks her abdomen forward, hurling an egg toward the ground. She does this until the ground is littered with her eggs.

1

Many of the eggs are collected by ants, but some land under vegetation and lie undisturbed. When a nymph hatches out, it looks like a large, fierce ant. It climbs up the nearest plant to enjoy its first meal of juicy, green leaves.

2

Did You Know?

● Macleay's specter is named after Alexander Macleay, who first described it. An avid insect collector, Macleay arrived in Australia from Britain in 1826 to be the Colonial Secretary of New South Wales. In his lifetime, he amassed a collection of 500,000 insects, now housed in a museum in the University of Sydney.

● A young Macleay's specter that loses a limb to a predator can grow a new leg the next time it molts. An adult may bring on a molt to generate a new limb, but it may not be as long as the one that it lost.

● The specter's ability to disguise itself as its host plant can mean that it becomes the unwitting victim of a hungry plant-eater.

● Macleay's specters are part of the group of insects called *phasmids*. This name comes from *phasm*, the Greek word for a phantom, or ghostly apparition. Other stick insects and leaf insects are also part of this group.

LEAF INSECT

Latin name: *Phyllium* species

ABDOMEN
This catches any breeze so that the whole insect sways gently, like a real leaf.

COLOR
On cool, gloomy days the skin darkens to absorb more of the sun's warmth. On hot, bright days it lightens, to absorb less.

ANTENNAS
These detect airborne scents and vibrations.

LEGS
The legs look like leaves that are almost completely nibbled away.

JAWS
The jaws are small but sharp and strong, for shredding and chewing leaves.

LEG-LOSS
A fully grown adult can shed a leg to save itself.

CLAW
Each leg ends in a small claw for clinging to smooth leaves.

This leaflike leaf-eater fools passing predators into thinking it is simply part of the lush jungle scenery. Birds and other enemies can't see a leaf insect at all unless it moves, so it doesn't, at least not during the day. Only at night does this tropical insect dare creep around the forest.

Each species has carefully adapted to blend into the foliage of the plant that they live on. They are superbly camouflaged in every detail, with veins and even caterpillar nibble-marks, just like real leaves.

HOW BIG IS IT?

BUG FACTS

LENGTH	2-4 in, depending on sex and species	*Phyllium* leaf insects live in the tropical rain forests of Sri Lanka, India, and south-eastern Asia, from Thailand south to Queensland in northern Australia, and in a few remote islands in the Pacific and Indian oceans —wherever there are food plants like rambutan, mango, and papaya.
DIET	Mainly the succulent green leaves of tropical plants, such as papaya	
LIFESPAN	Up to 3 years as a larva (grub); from a few weeks to several months as an adult	

1 Leaf insects have flat, finely veined extensions to their abdomens, legs, and wingcases, imitating leaves. One race of a particular species may look like pristine green leaves with purple edges.

Another race of the same species may look slightly different. The insects may have rust-colored markings, not purple ones. These imitate the reddish-brown fungus that often infects the edges of leaves. **2**

3 A third race of the same species may not be green at all, but brown, like dead leaves. They might even have ragged edges and holes in them, like leaves nibbled by caterpillars.

Did You Know?

 ● Leaf insects resemble leaves so closely that other insects often take bites out of their abdomens and wings, mistaking them for the leaves of their favorite food plants.

● In some species of leaf insect, the female is able to make a buzzing noise known as stridulation by vibrating her antennas (feelers) when she is harassed or alarmed.

● The ancient Chinese considered leaf insects to be real leaves that could walk away unharmed when special trees were felled.

● Although leaf insects taste their food carefully to ensure that it is edible, they cannot tell if it has been treated with insecticide. This has caused a great reduction in their numbers in many areas.

● In Malaysia, people have long kept leaf insects at home, believing they bring good luck. Leaf insects are now popular pets worldwide.

Moths, Bees, and Wasps

Moths, bees, and wasps are all flying insects. Like butterflies, moths belong to the "scaly winged" order of insects called Lepidoptera. Bees and wasps have skin-covered wings and belong to the order Hymenoptera.

Large moths may measure up to 12 inches from wingtip to wingtip. But one tiny moth measures less than $1/8$ inch. Like butterflies, moths are born from eggs as caterpillars or larvae. These larvae shed their skin several times before turning into insects with wings. Moths are "nocturnal," which means they mainly fly around at night. Moth food is mainly nectar, the sweet liquid they get from flowers.

Bees also collect nectar from flowers. They use the nectar to make honey. But bees do much more than make honey. They also do important work carrying pollen to trees to help them grow fruit. Unlike bees, wasps feed their young on meat. This means they have to be excellent hunters. Many types of wasps kill other bugs and insects to feed to their young. Spider wasps, for example, are experts at catching spiders. The bee-killer wasp feeds honeybees to her larvae while the unlucky bees are still alive.

Bees and wasps can be solitary like moths, which means that they live alone. Or they can be "social," which means they live together in a large hive with a big "queen bee" or "queen wasp" to lay the eggs.

DEATH'S HEAD HAWK MOTH

Latin name: *Acherontia atropos*

WINGS
In flight, the flapping wings make an audible buzzing sound.

ANTENNAS
These can pick up the smell of food or a mate from miles away.

DEATH'S HEAD
The markings vary widely, but on many moths they form the image of a skull.

UNDERWINGS
During the day, the moth rests, camouflaged by its dull upper wings. If disturbed, it startles intruders with a sudden flash of its colorful underwings.

EYES
Shortsighted, compound eyes are probably used to navigate by the light of the moon.

PROBOSCIS
If the moth is alarmed, it makes a loud squeaking sound by sucking air through the proboscis.

LEGS
Small hooks on the moth's legs help it cling to vertical surfaces.

With eerie skull-like markings on its back, the death's head hawk moth is a large, fast-flying night creature. You could be forgiven for mistaking this mighty moth for a bat as it flies into potato fields to lay its eggs. Its fat, crop-eating larvae are hated by farmers.

Night is also the ideal time for the hawk moth to steal the precious honey in a beehive, because many of the bees are resting. It repels any defending bees with some clever tricks.

HOW BIG IS IT?

Actual Size

BUG FACTS

LENGTH	Caterpillar 4³/₄ in; adult 1²/₃–2 in
WEIGHT	Adult ¹/₄ oz
WINGSPAN	4–4³/₄ in
DIET	Caterpillar: potato and tomato plant leaves, woody nightshade, privet, and thorn-apple; adult: honey, tree sap, and nectar
NUMBER OF EGGS	Up to 150
LIFESPAN	4–6 months from egg to adult; 2–3 months as adult

The death's head hawk moth is found through most of Africa, the Middle East, and southern Europe, but avoids the driest regions. It wanders farther north in summer to northern France and Britain, and occasionally reaches Iceland.

1 The sweet scent of honey draws a hawk moth to a hive. As the moth lands at the entrance and creeps inside, a few guard bees confront the intruder.

The moth has markings similar to those of the queen bee, and it makes a squeaking noise through its proboscis, which sounds just like the queen. The defensive bees turn away and the moth has the freedom of the hive.

2

3 Finding a comb of honey, the moth uses its proboscis to stab through the wax lid of a honey cell. The hungry moth steals a teaspoonful of honey in one sitting.

Did You Know?

● Beekeepers occasionally find death's head hawk moths embalmed in wax inside their beehives. So it seems that the moths occasionally fail to fool their intended victims—with fatal results.

● The death's head hawk moth was once called the bee robber or bee tiger because of its liking for honey.

● The death's head hawk moth is thought to be one of the world's fastest flying insects, achieving bursts of speed up to 34 miles per hour.

● If disturbed, the adult moth runs or hops around, squeaking loudly, while the caterpillar gnashes its mandibles to produce audible clicks.

FROTHING TIGER MOTH

Latin name: Family Arctiidae

HIND WINGS _____

When threatened, the moth raises its forewings to display the bright hind wings.

FROTH GLANDS _____

These glands emit yellow froth with a loud sizzling noise to alarm predators.

ANTENNAS

These detect scents in the air.

PROBOSCIS

The moth uses this long, curled tube to drink nectar from plants.

TYMBALS

A pair of drumlike organs detect the squeaks of bats, helping it avoid being eaten.

FOREWINGS

These have a pattern that helps disguise the moth in daytime.

Any hungry hunter that thinks a tiger moth offers an easy snack has a surprise in store. This crafty insect comes armed with a wide variety of amazing defenses. Tiger moth caterpillars take powerful poisons from the plants they eat, and the adults use bright colors to surprise their enemies and also to warn of their toxic contents.

If this fails, the moth starts to emit a sizzling yellow froth. This is usually enough to persuade any airborne hunter to seek an easier meal.

HOW BIG IS IT?

Actual Size

BUG FACTS

LENGTH	Up to 1 in	
WINGSPAN	Up to 2 in	
DIET	Larva: plants Adult: nectar	Tiger moths are found all over the world, except Antarctica, from the Arctic to tiny and remote Pacific islands. Their main requirement is that the habitat supports the various poisonous plants the caterpillars need to provide the ingredients for their chemical defenses.
DEFENSES	Toxins; shock tactics; bat signal-jamming device	
LIFESPAN	1 year	

1 With its built-in "sonar," a hunting bat detects a frothing tiger moth and swoops down. The killer's squeaks increase as it nears the target.

2 Hearing the bat's signal, the moth produces a sizzling foam. The puzzled bat veers away.

Did You Know?

● The mechanism to block a bat's echolocation system is automatic. When a particular frequency of bat squeaks is received by the moth's sound-detectors, it triggers muscle contractions that activate click-producing organs on the abdomen.

● After foaming in response to a threatening predator, the frothing tiger moth calmly extends its long proboscis and drinks the foam from its body to conserve moisture.

● Not all predators are repelled by the frothing tiger moth's foam. Birds such as flycatchers and cuckoos seem to be immune to the fluid's smell, taste, and toxins.

● Some tiger moths scuttle along the ground so rapidly that they are sometimes mistaken for mice.

● The tiger moth family name Arctiidae comes from the Greek word for "bear," a reference to the hairy "wooly bear" caterpillars.

PUSS MOTH

Latin name: *Cerula vinula*

EYESPOTS

Two large, staring false eyes help scare predators away. _____

HEAD _____

The tough head bears strong jaws for chomping through the leaves of food trees, as well as a pair of tiny antennas (feelers) and a cluster of simple eyes.

TRUE LEGS _____

Each of the first three segments bears a pair of legs. They play only a minor part in walking. They are used instead to hold leaves firmly while the larva munches.

"TAILS"

The larva can push out two long, tail-like projections from its rear end. The larva waves these menacingly when threatened.

"SADDLE"

This purple-black blotch on the back helps camouflage the larva from enemies such as birds.

PROLEGS

There are four pairs of soft, fleshy prolegs. They have tiny hooks that give a strong grip on the leaves.

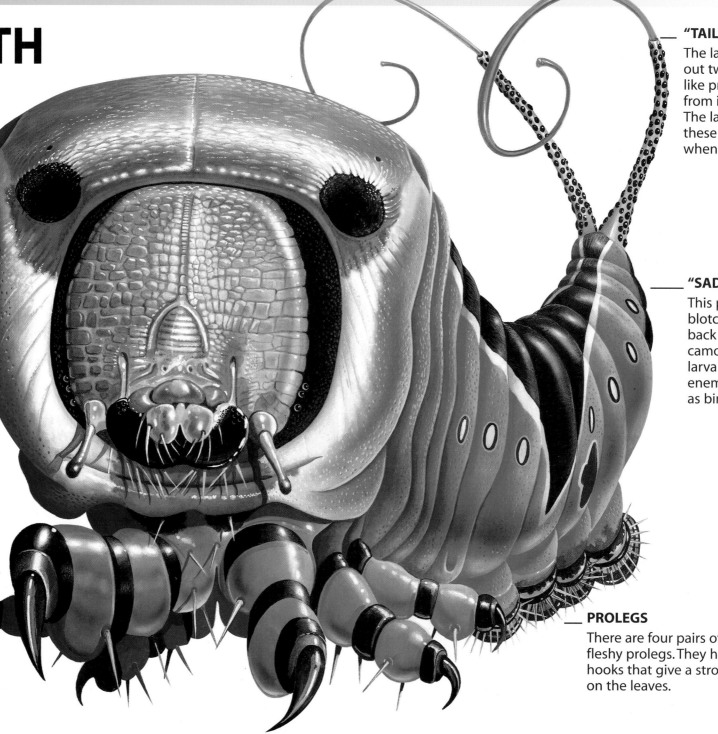

Every day in spring, birds grab caterpillars by the thousand to feed their hungry nestlings. So in order to stay off the menu, the puss moth larva pulls a face. It pulls its head into its forequarters, which rise and swell menacingly. Meanwhile, two red-tipped, whiplike tails spring from its rear, waving scarily over its back. This weird effect is enough to spook many attackers.

HOW BIG IS IT?

The larva is well camouflaged as it chews through the foliage of a willow or some other tree. Its plump body is leaf-colored, while the dark "saddle" on its back gives it the look of a rolled-up leaf.

1

By late summer or early fall, the larva turns purple. It makes a cocoon to surround itself while it changes into an adult.

2

When it is ready, the adult emerges from the cocoon. It dries its wings before taking flight.

3

BUG FACTS

SIZE	Caterpillar: up to 2$\frac{1}{2}$ in; adult: wingspan up to 3$\frac{1}{6}$ in (female), 2$\frac{1}{4}$ in (male)
DIET	Eats leaves of willow, sallow, poplar, and aspen trees
LIFESPAN	About 1 year as caterpillar; adult lives only for about 4 months

The puss moth lives across Europe, as far east as Siberia, southeast to Russia and Japan, and south to North Africa. It likes woods, hedges, and riverbanks where the caterpillar's food trees are common.

Did You Know?

● Puss moths can be spotted in towns and cities, where they are attracted to streetlights and porch lights as they fly around at night.

● A small, dark spot appears at the top of each puss moth egg shortly after it is laid. This looks like the hole made by a baby caterpillar when it leaves the egg, fooling some birds into thinking their intended meal is no longer worth eating.

● In striking contrast to the full-grown caterpillar, the young stage is much duller, blackish-brown. Its body bears a pair of conspicuous earlike projections behind the head.

● To help ensure that he alone is the father of a female's offspring, a male moth spends many hours mating with her. Later, she may no longer attract other males because the special scents she produced for this purpose may have evaporated—or her eggs may have matured and she is ready to lay them at once.

GREEN LACEWING

Latin name: Family Chrysopidae

EXOSKELETON

This is the larva's outer skin, which hardens soon after hatching. It is shed three times as the larva grows.

HAIRS

Sharp hairs sprout from the lacewing larva's body.

LEGS

The larva has six sturdy legs tipped with tiny claws for clambering over leaves.

ANTENNAS

The antennas have scent receptors to help the larva home in on a target.

JAWS

The larva grips a victim with its curved jaws while it pushes its mouthparts into the soft body.

EYES

The eyes are sensitive to the movements of both predators and prey.

MOUTHPARTS

The larva's hollow mouthparts pump digestive juices into its victims and then suck them dry.

The offspring of this delicate insect are friend to farmer and gardener alike. Green lacewing larvae feast on troublesome plant pests and then wear the empty bodies on their back like a gruesome coat. This isn't showing off—the coat acts as camouflage.

Green lacewing larvae are built to kill and feed and they're especially fond of aphids. Wherever these sap-sucking pests may swarm, the hungry hunter is hard at work with its sickle-shaped jaws and lethal venom.

HOW BIG IS IT?

x2

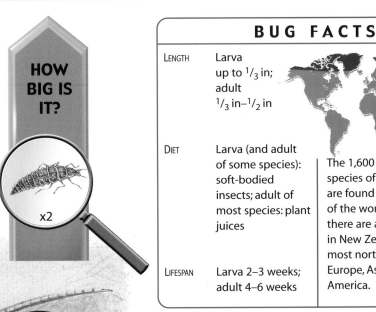

BUG FACTS

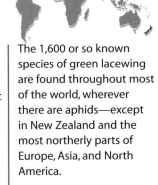

LENGTH	Larva up to ¹/₃ in; adult ¹/₃ in–¹/₂ in
DIET	Larva (and adult of some species): soft-bodied insects; adult of most species: plant juices
LIFESPAN	Larva 2–3 weeks; adult 4–6 weeks

The 1,600 or so known species of green lacewing are found throughout most of the world, wherever there are aphids—except in New Zealand and the most northerly parts of Europe, Asia, and North America.

A colony of aphids feasts on a juicy leaf. A green lacewing larva grabs one of the pests between its huge jaws and gives the target a shot of paralyzing venom.

1

2

The aphid hangs helplessly as the venom begin to liquefy its insides. The larva sucks up the mush using its tubular mouthparts, leaving the prey a dry, empty husk.

The lacewing larva hooks the dead aphid's body onto its back. There it becomes another part of its "coat of many corpses." The hunter is soon bearing down on its next hapless victim.

3

Did You Know?

● The green lacewing larva will travel almost 100 feet to find food. In its brief life, the predator can consume 250 leafhopper nymphs, 600 aphids, 11,000 spider mites, 3,800 scale insects, or 6,500 insect eggs.

● Adult lacewings are active at night, and are preyed on by bats. Some adults have a bat-avoidance mechanism: special receptor cells in the wings that detect a bat's calls.

● The larva of one green lacewing species disguises itself as its wooly aphid prey. Ants "milk" aphids for a sugary liquid called honeydew that they secrete and, in return, protect them from predators. To escape the attention of the ants, the lacewing larva covers itself in a white wax that it scrapes off the aphids' backs. The killer then feeds on the aphids without being noticed by the ants.

● Some aphids secrete a sticky substance designed to block the lacewing larva's hollow mouthparts.

LOBSTER MOTH

Latin name: *Staurophagus fagi*

HUMPS
Double-pointed humps on the grub's back make it appear more scary.

"TAIL"
The flattened, swollen "tail" gives the caterpillar its lobsterlike appearance.

MOUTH
The strong mouthparts can easily chomp through succulent tree leaves.

LEGS
The extra-long second and third pair of legs help it to mimic an ant or a spider to scare its enemies.

PROLEGS
Five pairs of "false legs," called prolegs, support the rear of the body.

The lobster moth caterpillar is a master of disguise. When it first hatches out it resembles an ant, and few predators want to tangle with an ant so they tend to stay away. As it gets bigger, the caterpillar turns reddish-brown and grows a tail, giving it the lobsterlike shape from which it gets its name. When threatened, it arches its tail over its back to display stinglike spikes. It also raises its head and shakes its long legs like an spider. For most predators, this odd-looking insect is too frightening to attack, and they leave it well alone.

HOW BIG IS IT?

Actual Size

BUG FACTS

SIZE	Adult wingspan 2–2³/₄ in; caterpillar up to 3 in long	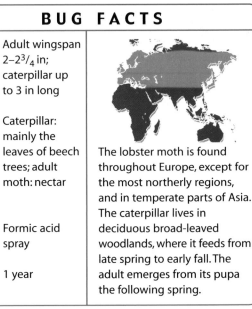
DIET	Caterpillar: mainly the leaves of beech trees; adult moth: nectar	
DEFENSES	Formic acid spray	
LIFESPAN	1 year	

The lobster moth is found throughout Europe, except for the most northerly regions, and in temperate parts of Asia. The caterpillar lives in deciduous broad-leaved woodlands, where it feeds from late spring to early fall. The adult emerges from its pupa the following spring.

1 A lobster moth caterpillar is crawling along a branch when it sees an approaching squirrel. At once, the insect raises its head and tail and waggles its long front legs in a warning gesture.

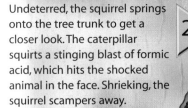

Undeterred, the squirrel springs onto the tree trunk to get a closer look. The caterpillar squirts a stinging blast of formic acid, which hits the shocked animal in the face. Shrieking, the squirrel scampers away. **2**

Did You Know?

● The adult lobster moth is exceptionally hairy. This provides protection against many insect-eating birds, which tend to avoid prey that is unpleasant to swallow. The cuckoo is one of the few birds undeterred by the furry covering.

● During laboratory studies of the lobster moth caterpillar, individuals kept close together have been seen to bite off each other's legs.

● The adult lobster moth flies mainly at night and spends most of the day resting on the trunk of a tree or on a branch. The moth's dull, mottled coloring and the shape of its wings helps to disguise the insect as part of the bark of the tree.

● The lobster moth's camouflage varies according to pollution levels in the region. Lobster moths living in southern Ireland are lighter in color than those found in more heavily polluted areas of the British Isles, such as southern England.

SAND WASP

Latin name: *Ammophila* species

EYES
Large complex eyes are vital for hunting, and recognizing landmarks.

JAWS
Two powerful pincer jaws are the wasp's "hands." It uses the pincers for digging and carrying.

ABDOMEN
At night, the male wasp rests with his abdomen pointing up in the air.

WAIST
The tiny waist is highly flexible. This allows the wasp to bend around tight corners in its burrow.

FORELEGS
Long hairs on the inside of the forelegs help it dig.

A sand wasp performs some impressive tasks. It has excellent engineering skills and cleverly camouflages the nests it builds. It also has an amazing memory and can capture prey far larger than itself. After capturing a plump grub, the female injects it with paralyzing venom. She drags the grub along the ground and buries it in a nest with one of her eggs. She builds separate nests for each of her offspring, and returns to the nests to keep them supplied with fresh flesh.

HOW BIG IS IT?

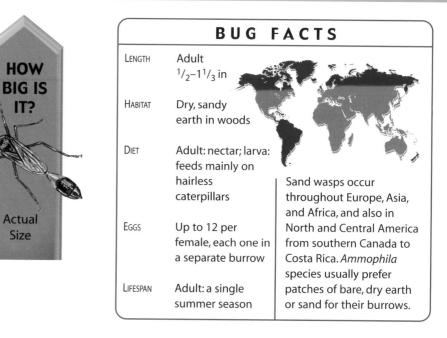

Actual Size

BUG FACTS

LENGTH	Adult $\frac{1}{2}$–$1\frac{1}{3}$ in
HABITAT	Dry, sandy earth in woods
DIET	Adult: nectar; larva: feeds mainly on hairless caterpillars
EGGS	Up to 12 per female, each one in a separate burrow
LIFESPAN	Adult: a single summer season

Sand wasps occur throughout Europe, Asia, and Africa, and also in North and Central America from southern Canada to Costa Rica. *Ammophila* species usually prefer patches of bare, dry earth or sand for their burrows.

1 A sand wasp has just paralyzed a large, juicy caterpillar. She grabs hold of its head, and drags it to one of her nests.

She pulls the caterpillar into her burrow and lays her egg on its body. After climbing out, she seals the entrance with sand and small stones. **2**

Inside the sealed burrow, the egg hatches into a tiny white larva. It soon begins to munch on the helpless caterpillar, slowly eating it alive. Eventually the caterpillar dies, but the mother's venom helps preserve it. The larva keeps eating it until she brings a fresh victim. **3**

Did You Know?

● The female sand wasp drags caterpillars of up to ten times her own weight to the larval burrow, and she also steals caterpillars from other wasps' nests if given the chance.

● A burrow stocked with one big caterpillar is more likely to produce a female wasp larva than one that contains several small caterpillars.

● If the female wasp encounters an ant while digging her burrow, she attacks, nipping at the ant with her jaws or picking it up and dropping it a few inches away.

● Male sand wasps are only half the weight of females and take no part in family life after mating.

BEE-KILLER WASP

Latin name: *Philanthus triangulum*

EYES

The compound eyes are made up of many tiny lenses. It may be that each lens adds a small part to the overall picture seen by the wasp, but experts can't be sure.

JAWS

The powerful jaws, are used to tunnel into sandy soil.

STINGER

This sharp, hollow tub pierces the honeybee's body and pumps in venom.

ANTENNAS

These are used to feel the wasp's surroundings and detect airborne smells and vibrations.

FOREFEET

The forefeet are equipped with strong spines that shovel sand behind as the female digs her burrow.

This frighteningly efficient hunter has just one mission in life—to nourish her larvae on living flesh. To capture her quarry the female bee-killer lurks close to flowers, knowing her industrious prey, the honeybee, will never be far away.

Most predators avoid honeybees because their stripy markings show they are equipped with a vicious sting. But the bee-killer wasp has no such fears. She patrols busily in search of victims to grab and imprisons her captives in underground cells to form a living larder for her young.

HOW BIG IS IT?

Actual Size

BUG FACTS

SIZE	Female up to $^4/_5$ in; male up to $^1/_2$ in
DIET	Adult: nectar and pollen; larvae: honeybees
WEAPONS	Venom-primed tail-sting
LIFESPAN	Adult: from July to September

The bee-killer wasp is widespread throughout most of Europe, except for the coldest areas in the far north. The wasp is very common in south and central Europe, where the populations of honeybees, so important as food for its young, are most numerous.

A bee-killer wasp hovers slightly downwind of a honeybee. She smells the air to check the scent of her prey. Once she is sure it is a honeybee, the wasp swoops in to strike.

1

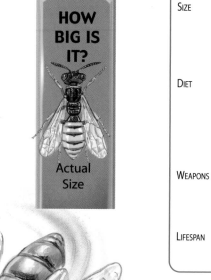

2

The wasp grabs the quarry with her long legs. She takes great care to avoid the bee's deadly sting as the two enemies tumble downward.

The attacker plunges her great sting into the bee. Once her prize is secure, the wasp sucks up the nectar that is forced out of the bee's mouth. Energized by this refreshing drink, she flies off with the helpless prey.

3

Did You Know?

● The female bee-killer wasp sucks up the blood that oozes out of her victim's wounds. The proteins in the blood are a useful supplement to her otherwise vegetarian diet.

● Unlike its relative, the common wasp (*Vespula vulgaris*), the bee-killer spends most of its time alone. However, hundreds of the insects sometimes huddle in the evenings on branches and blades of grass to spend the night asleep in a clump.

● After stinging a honeybee, the wasp kneads the victim with her legs, to spread her paralyzing toxins quickly through the quarry's body.

● Although the bee-killer wasp hunts and feeds its larvae on honeybees only, scientists have discovered that the larvae are happy to eat a wide range of different insects.

● The female bee-killer attracts a mate with scent secretions emitted from glands on her abdomen.

PAPER WASP

Latin name: *Polybia, Polistes, Melanogaster,* and other species

EYES
Multifaceted compound eyes provide good color vision.

ANTENNAS
The antennas help the wasp find new food sources and detect chemical signals from other wasps.

STING
The sting is loaded with venom and can be used repeatedly.

HEAD
The large head contains one of the best brains in the insect world. It is programmed with the advanced skills needed to hunt prey and build nests.

LEGS
The strong front legs grip a victim while the jaws get to work.

JAWS
The jaws are tough enough to chew up wood and crunch into the wasp's insect prey.

The paper wasp is one of nature's finest architects. Worker wasps scrape wood fibers from dead branches, which they mix with saliva or water to form a wet paper pulp for building their nests with. Unfortunately, their painful stings make paper wasps unwelcome neighbors. Getting rid of a colony that has moved in next to your home is no easy matter. Any threat to the nest triggers an attack by thousands of irate defenders.

HOW BIG IS IT?

Actual Size

A man is alarmed by a wasp nest that has appeared beneath the eaves of his home. He grabs a heavy stick and tries to knock it down.

1

Defending their colony against the attack, the wasps dive at the man's face. He is stung many times as he flees in panic.

2

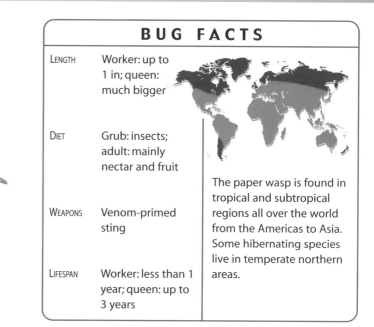

BUG FACTS

LENGTH	Worker: up to 1 in; queen: much bigger
DIET	Grub: insects; adult: mainly nectar and fruit
WEAPONS	Venom-primed sting
LIFESPAN	Worker: less than 1 year; queen: up to 3 years

The paper wasp is found in tropical and subtropical regions all over the world from the Americas to Asia. Some hibernating species live in temperate northern areas.

Did You Know?

● In many species of paper wasp the queen maintains control by stopping the other females from becoming fertile. She does this by "broadcasting" a special chemical called "queen substance." As she ages she gets less effective at doing this, until she is deposed. In some wasp species, the queen stays boss by brute force. Only the toughest, fiercest female rules the roost.

● Wasps build a nest quickly, with different workers specializing in particular jobs. They know their stuff; a Polybia nest can stay in use for up to 25 years, far longer than the lifespan of any individual wasp.

● The stalk of a paper wasp's nest is coated in a lacquer that contains ant repellent. This deters most ants, but has no effect on army ants.

● In hot weather the workers may keep the nest cool by gathering near the entrance and fanning their wings to drive air through it.

SPIDER WASP

Latin name: Subfamily Pompilinae

WINGS
Powerful wings help the spider wasp to fly while carrying a big spider.

LEGS
These have hooked claws for grappling with spiders.

EYES
Huge compound eyes give the wasp excellent eyesight for an insect. It certainly has better eyesight than most spiders.

STING
The sting injects a paralyzing venom.

ANTENNAS
Scent receptors on the antennas help the wasp locate a victim's lair.

MOUTHPARTS
Strong, sharp mouthparts make useful weapons and tools for digging.

Usually it's the spiders that catch insects in their webs. However, a particular type of spider wasp turns the tables on the spider and uses this spider's own web to capture it.

First the wasp tricks the spider into leaving the safety of its web. Then, skillfully avoiding the spider's fangs, the wasp curls her tail under the spider's body to drive her sting deep into its body. From then on, the spider is just baby food.

HOW BIG IS IT?

Actual Size

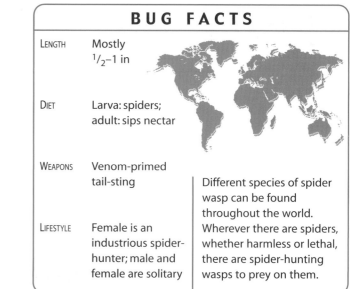

BUG FACTS

LENGTH	Mostly 1/2–1 in
DIET	Larva: spiders; adult: sips nectar
WEAPONS	Venom-primed tail-sting
LIFESTYLE	Female is an industrious spider-hunter; male and female are solitary

Different species of spider wasp can be found throughout the world. Wherever there are spiders, whether harmless or lethal, there are spider-hunting wasps to prey on them.

1 A female spider wasp discovers a fat orb spider in its web. The wasp plucks at the silk threads. The spider immediately tries to escape by spinning a line and dropping to the ground. Somehow, the wasp doesn't get caught up in the sticky web, and gives chase.

2 The wasp nips down the line. When she catches up with her victim, she wrestles it to the ground. After a brief battle, she plunges her tail-sting deep into the spider's belly. The fight is over.

Did You Know?

 ● When the wasp grub eats its living food store, it instinctively avoids the vital organs to keep the spider alive for as long as possible.

● Some spider wasps stock their larders with several small spiders rather than one large one. They have to be careful to remember the exact location of each burrow, so they can return to it with each new victim.

● The green lynx spider pluckily spits venom at wasp spiders, but this defense doesn't always work.

● The giant *Pepsis* spider wasp of the Americas is commonly known as the tarantula hawk because it preys on enormous, hairy, deadly "tarantulas."

● Scientists are not sure if the spider wasp's victims suffer while they are eaten alive. The wasp's venom may plunge the spider into such a deep "coma" that it feels nothing at all as the grub munches away at it. We can only hope so.

ICHNEUMON WASP

Latin name: Subfamilies *Rhyssinae* & others

ABDOMEN
The abdomen is segmented for flexibility, so the wasp can push down on its drilling tube.

WINGS
The long, slender wings make the wasp a fast flier.

ANTENNAS
The long, jointed antennas are equipped with sensors to detect the scent of grubs and nectar.

LEGS
Long legs let the insect rear up high above the wood to insert its drill.

MOUTHPARTS
The adult has tough jaws so it can gnaw its way out of the timber when it hatches from the pupa.

MARKINGS
This species has black-and-yellow markings, to make enemies think it can sting like other wasps can (it can't).

OVIPOSITOR
The egg-laying ovipositor is like a doctor's needle tipped with a drill. When not in use, the organs stick out behind the wasp.

The slender female ichneumon wasp sips nectar from flowers, but her young eat their way through the juicy bodies of live insect grubs.

The mother injects an egg into an insect grub or lays it on the grub's skin. When the egg hatches, the infant wasp slowly eats its victim alive. Some species of ichneumon wasp can locate grubs deep inside trees. The accuracy with which they locate the grubs is uncanny, and scientists are still trying to figure out exactly how they do it.

HOW BIG IS IT?

Actual Size

BUG FACTS

LENGTH	Head and body $1/8$–$1^2/3$ in, depending on species; the female's ovipositor can be several times longer	
DIET	Adult: sips nectar from flowers; grub: eats beetle and other insect larvae	Ichneumon wasps live all over the world, except Antarctica and the High Arctic. They are found wherever there are insect grubs for their larvae to tuck into and nectar for the adult wasps to drink.
LIFESPAN	Up to 3 years	

A female ichneumon wasp drills through the bark of a tree and straight into a tunneling grub. It lays an egg inside the larva.

1

As soon as the wasp grub hatches it starts chomping its way through its tunneling grub. Once the grub is fully grown it finally kills its host by devouring the vital organs. It then bursts out of the body.

2

Did You Know?

● More than 20,000 species of ichneumon wasp are known around the world, and scientists think there could be as many as 30,000 more waiting to be discovered.

● Ichneumon wasps are also known (wrongly) as ichneumon flies.

● The eggs of some ichneumon wasps are infected with special viruses that attack the host grubs' immune system to stop it from destroying the feeding wasp larvae.

● For some strange reason, *Rhyssa persuasoria*, a common ichneumon wasp in Europe, was once called "the persuasive burglar" in many areas.

● Some ichneumon wasps aren't equipped to drill through timber. Instead, the female lurks nearby while the female of another species does all the hard work, then slips her own egg down the hole. When the egg hatches, the larva kills its rival and eats the host grub itself.

ROLLING WASP

Latin name: Family Tiphiidae

ANTENNAS

Scent receptors on the antennas help the male find a female to mate.

EYES

The large compound eyes help the female wasp to find the hidden lair of her next victim.

WINGS

All males fly. Some species have wingless females, which hunt "on foot."

MOUTHPARTS

The adult wasp has powerful mouthparts. But it feeds mainly on sugary foods such as nectar and honeydew.

CLAWS

The male wasp uses his hooked claws to hold on to the female when mating.

STING

The rolling wasp's extra-long sting is loaded with a big dose of powerful paralyzing venom.

Male and female rolling wasps believe in sharing out the chores. The male rolling wasp spends his day visiting flowers and collecting nectar for himself and his partner. The female devotes her time to life-or-death battles with killer grubs. Armed with her paralyzing sting, this slender wasp is an efficient and fearless hunter of fat, ferocious beetle grubs. She then uses the grubs as living larders for her developing young.

HOW BIG IS IT?

Actual Size

BUG FACTS

LENGTH	1/6–12 in; size depends on species
DIET	Adult eats nectar; larva eats insect grubs
WEAPONS	Tail-sting primed with paralyzing venom
LIFESPAN	A few weeks as an adult

There are at least 1,500 species of rolling wasp. They are found in all but the coldest areas of the world, wherever there is nectar to drink and grubs on which to feed their larvae.

1 A hungry tiger beetle grub is lying in wait inside its burrow. It tries to capture a female rolling wasp, but its powerful jaws can't close on her slim waist.

2 The wasp arches her body and stabs her sting into the grub's throat. Her sting pumps paralyzing chemicals into the grub. She drags the larva into her lair and lays an egg on its body. Sealing up the hole, she goes in search of another juicy victim.

Did You Know?

● Males are rare in some rolling wasp species, because unmated females often lay eggs, which results in all-female offspring. This process, known as *parthenogenesis*, is also seen in insects such as aphids.

● Among rolling wasps that have to mate, the bigger male often picks up the wingless female and flies around with her. This enables him to check on her breeding condition. If she is too light—and so probably not up to the job—he drops her.

● Some rolling wasps target garden pests, so they can be used as pest control agents—just like the ladybugs and lacewings, which gardeners buy to clear up greenflies.

● Some parasitic wasps attack flies, caterpillars, crickets, cicadas, bees, and even other wasps. But the most intrepid by far is the tarantula hawk wasp (subfamily Pepsinae), which wrestles giant spiders before paralyzing them with its sting.

HORNET

Latin name: *Vespa crabo*

SENSES

Antennas test the air for traces of food. Big compound eyes detect the small movements of prey.

JAWS

Chopping, slicing jaws chew prey to a pulp.

LEGS

The hornet grabs prey with its strong legs and clawed feet.

WINGS

The two pairs of wings beat powerfully for top speed. They make the hornet's familiar loud whining hum.

COLORS

Bold yellow and brown patterns warn birds and other predators to stay away.

STING

The sting is made of two spikes and a tube through which the venom flows.

Bigger and even meaner than its cousin the common wasp, the hornet is a very aggressive creature. When angry, it flies straight at you, whining viciously and flashing its wickedly sharp tail-sting.

All around the hornets' nest hundreds of worker hornets are kept busy fetching fresh meat for the nest's grubs. Worker hornets hunt relentlessly during every dry, daylight hour and any small insect that strays into the killing area is dicing with death.

HOW BIG IS IT?

Actual Size

BUG FACTS

LENGTH	Queen: 1–1⅓ in; workers: ⅘–1 in
DIET	Insects, nectar, sap, and other plant juices
TYPICAL ATTACK	Stings once, but sometimes more
VENOM	Very painful and causes swelling
LIFESPAN	Queen over 5 years; workers and males up to 1 year

The hornet *Vespa crabro* lives across southern England, in mainland Europe and Scandinavia, and through central Asia as far east as Mongolia. Closely related species occur in North America.

1 A worker hornet pounces on a horsefly. It stops it from escaping with a lethal injection of venom.

3 The hornet chews the lifeless body of the fly to an easy-to-swallow mush, then flies back to the nest. It regurgitates the warm mashed remains straight into the mouth of a fat, wriggling grub.

2 The hornet ruthlessly snips off the creature's wings, legs, and head using its powerful jaws.

Did You Know?

● Extracts of hornet venom have been used in medical trials to treat people with high blood pressure.

● The activity of hornets in a nest can raise the temperature inside by as much as 59°F. If the nest overheats, the workers gather at the entrance and fan their wings to ventilate it. They also dab water over the cells to cool the developing larvae.

● When hornet larvae are hungry, they rub their bodies on the sides of their cells to tell the waiting workers.

● The hornet builds its nest—a honeycomb of hexagonal cells—from dead wood that it has first chewed into a pulp that can be easily molded.

COMMON WASP

Latin name: *Vespula vulgaris*

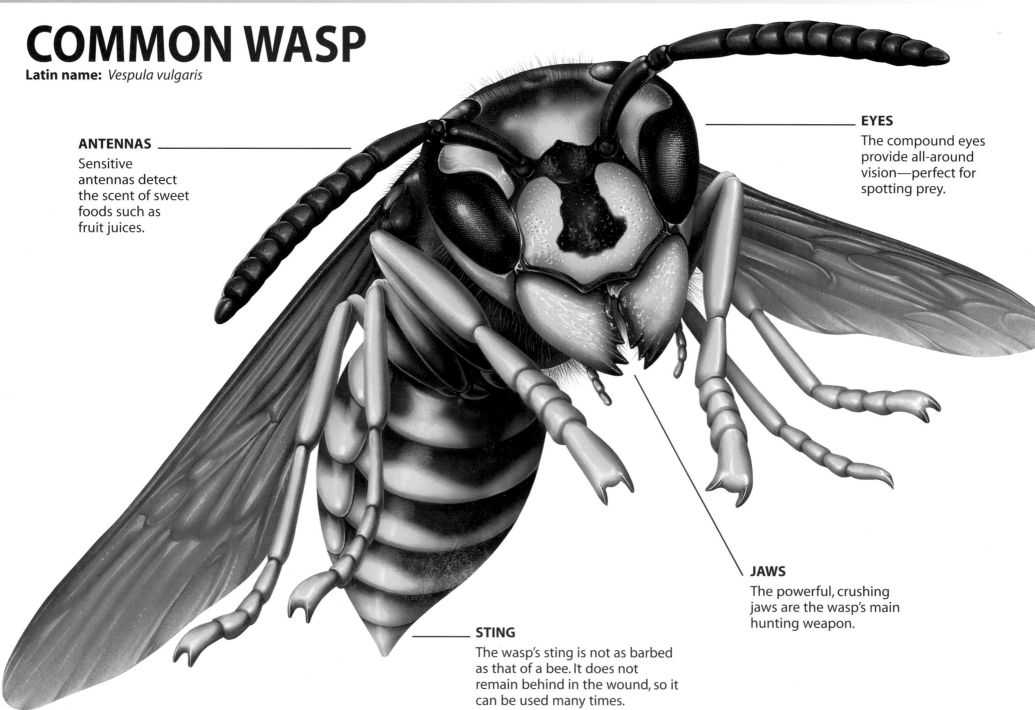

ANTENNAS

Sensitive antennas detect the scent of sweet foods such as fruit juices.

EYES

The compound eyes provide all-around vision—perfect for spotting prey.

JAWS

The powerful, crushing jaws are the wasp's main hunting weapon.

STING

The wasp's sting is not as barbed as that of a bee. It does not remain behind in the wound, so it can be used many times.

Common wasps are sociable, hardworking creatures that spend their days building ingenious nests and collecting food for their grubs. But for some, the sight of these striped insects can provoke a sense of terror. The wasp's love of sugar makes it a potential danger if it finds its way into your drink. If you don't spot it, the insect could enter your mouth and sting your tongue, making it swell and stopping you from breathing.

Attracted by the smell of a fizzy soda at a picnic, a wasp finds its way into the can and becomes trapped inside.

1

HOW BIG IS IT?

Actual Size

BUG FACTS

LENGTH	Queen: $1/2$–$4/5$ in, worker: $1/3$–$1/2$ in	
DIET	Plant juices, insects, and carrion	
WEAPONS	Strong jaws and tail-sting	The common wasp probably originally lived only in Europe, but it has been accidentally spread around the globe by humans, and is now found throughout much of Asia, as well as Australia, and North and Central America.
LIFESPAN	Queen: 13–14 months; worker: a few weeks	

2 Unaware that the wasp is struggling inside her can, a girl takes a long drink. The wasp floats into her mouth. In panic, the wasp stings her many times on the back of her tongue.

3 The girl's tongue begins to swell inside her mouth. She risks being suffocated. She must get to a hospital at once or she may die.

Did You Know?

● Male wasps do not help out in the colony. They can spend their time idly sipping nectar from flowers—just waiting to mate with any young queen wasps that emerge from the nest.

● In hot countries, wasp colonies do not die off in the winter, so they are able to survive for many years, growing steadily bigger and bigger each year.

● If wasp grubs die in the nest, the adults recycle them by feeding them to the grubs that are still living.

● The wasp's warning colors are mimicked by some flies, which then avoid being eaten. Predators such as birds are scared off by the stripes.

● Anglers use wasp nests and grubs to catch a fish called chub. They poison a wasp's nest, take out a few grubs for the hook, and pour boiling water on the nest to make a mash. Thrown in a river, this drives chub into a frenzy.

KILLER BEE

Latin name: *Apis mellifera scutellata*

WINGS ————————
The wings vibrate so
rapidly that they make
an audible buzz.

ABDOMEN
The stripes act as a bold
warning to predators.
The stripes are copied by
some harmless insects as
a defense mechanism.

JAWS
Bees use their jaws like
hands to build their nests.

STING
This is an egg-
laying organ in
the colony queen,
but in worker bees
it has evolved into
a sting.

Killer bees are technically known as Africanized honeybees, because they are a cross between the ferocious African honeybee and European honeybees. This African race was originally imported to Brazil, and have now swept across the Americas.

Killer bees attack at the slightest alarm. Loud noises, movement, and even unusual smells can set them off. A stinging bee releases a special scent to attract reinforcements, so victims are rapidly surrounded by a huge swarm and can be stung thousands of times.

HOW BIG IS IT?

Actual Size

BUG FACTS

LENGTH	Queen: up to $4/5$ in; worker: up to $1/2$ in	
DIET	Nectar, pollen, and honey	
LIFESPAN	Queen: 4–5 years; worker: 20 days	
EGGS LAID BY QUEEN	Up to 2,000 per day; 2 million in a lifetime	
COLONY SIZE	Up to 80,000	
VENOM	Injected by tail sting	
FATAL ATTACK	Normally requires 300 or more stings	

Originally from southern Africa, the introduced African honeybee has spread across South America, interbreeding with local bees. These "killer" bees are found in Argentina, northern Mexico, California, and Texas.

A killer bee lands on a human. It plunges its sting into the skin.

1

The bee pulls away. The sting is torn from its body, releasing a *pheromone* (special smell) that attracts other bees to the scene.

2

3 Muscles around the sting continue working for up to 60 seconds. They force the sting deeper into the skin and pump venom into the wound.

Did You Know?

● Killer bees have been known to attack people who come within half a mile of their nest, and may chase intruders for up to 2,500 feet.

● During a ferocious, 15-minute attack in Bisbee, Arizona, killer bees stung pedestrians, motorists, dogs, and even pigeons in flight.

● The killer bee can only fly at 4 miles per hour, so many victims manage to run away. Serious casualties tend to be those with limited mobility.

● Killer bees are superb honeymakers. In the United States, hives of European bees make about 53 pounds of honey per season; Africanized bees produce up to 198 pounds.

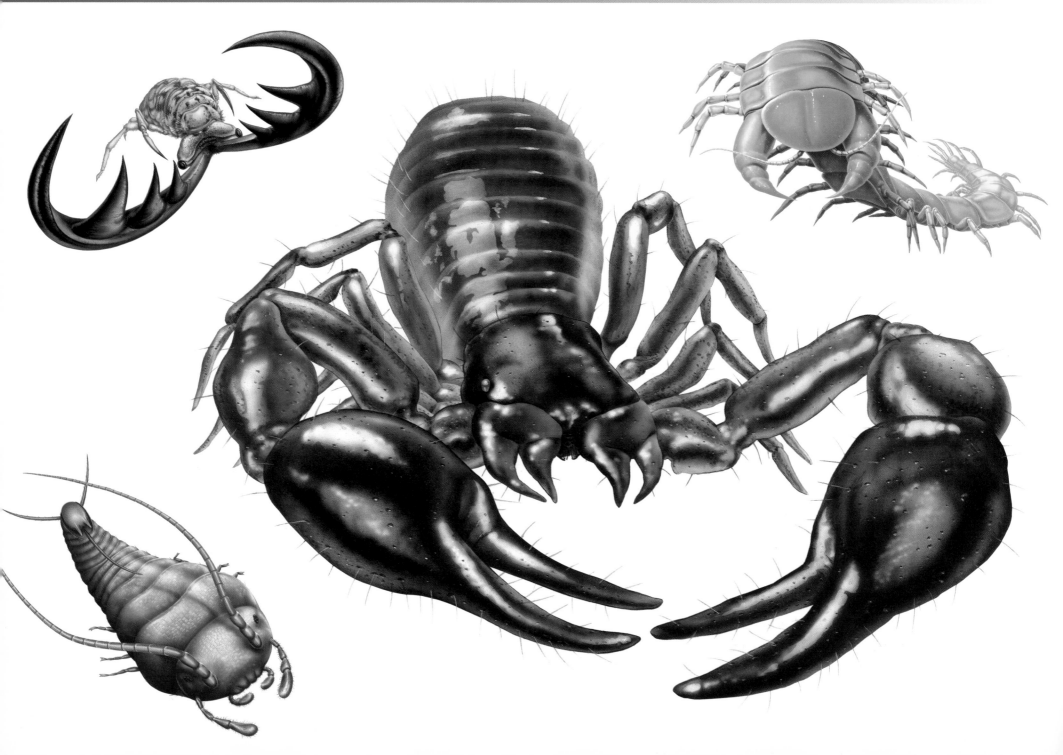

Other Creepy-Crawlies

People call insects "creepy-crawlies" because they are afraid of them and they don't like the way they scuttle around. If you see an insect of any kind, it's much better to leave it alone—if you do, it won't sting or bite you.

Some creepy-crawly creatures, like the antlion or the bark scorpion, have powerful hooks or claws. The antlion's hooks are really jaws with sharp points. The antlion uses these to push poison into its victim before eating it. But it's only dangerous if you are the size of an ant! Other bugs and creepy-crawlies can be more of a threat to humans. The bark scorpion has a long poison-tipped tail, although it will only attack if you take it by surprise.

Another creepy-crawly, the giant centipede, also has poisonous claws. The name "centipede" means

"one hundred feet" but this is just a rough guess, so don't try counting them! The false scorpion looks like the deadly spiderlike scorpion, but it's much smaller and doesn't have the scorpion's tail. Even so, its claws contain poison that can kill its victims.

Other creepy-crawlies can be dangerous in other ways. For instance, if wood termites nibble away at wooden floorboards, they may break when you tread on them and give you a nasty fall. But few of these mini-monsters are very interested in humans—they usually prefer to pick on creatures their own size.

TAILLESS WHIP SCORPION
Latin name: Suborder Amblypygi

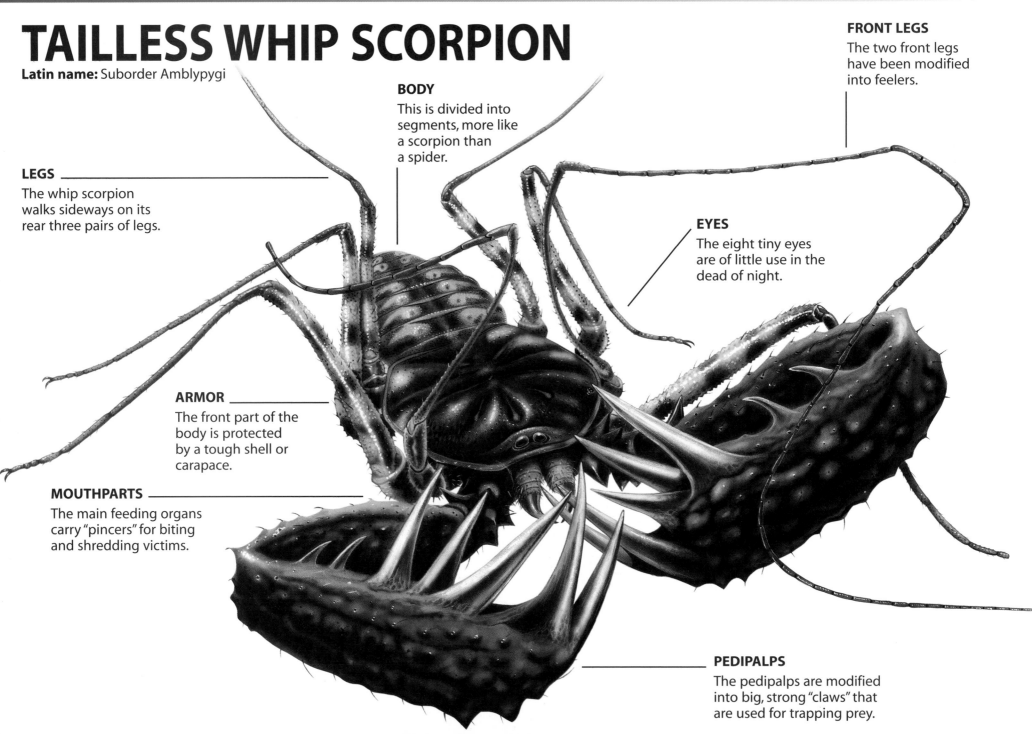

FRONT LEGS
The two front legs have been modified into feelers.

BODY
This is divided into segments, more like a scorpion than a spider.

LEGS
The whip scorpion walks sideways on its rear three pairs of legs.

EYES
The eight tiny eyes are of little use in the dead of night.

ARMOR
The front part of the body is protected by a tough shell or carapace.

MOUTHPARTS
The main feeding organs carry "pincers" for biting and shredding victims.

PEDIPALPS
The pedipalps are modified into big, strong "claws" that are used for trapping prey.

As night falls, the tailless whip scorpion creeps from its hiding place and sets off to hunt. Although it's related to spiders and scorpions, the creature doesn't need a web or venom to subdue its prey. With its huge spiny "claws" and scuttling run, it can pounce on prey in an instant and tear its victims to pieces. This powerful beast often lurks in a crevice with only its long, sensitive legs sticking out, like trip wires.

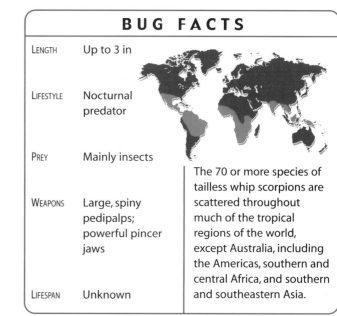

HOW BIG IS IT?

BUG FACTS

LENGTH	Up to 3 in
LIFESTYLE	Nocturnal predator
PREY	Mainly insects
WEAPONS	Large, spiny pedipalps; powerful pincer jaws
LIFESPAN	Unknown

The 70 or more species of tailless whip scorpions are scattered throughout much of the tropical regions of the world, except Australia, including the Americas, southern and central Africa, and southern and southeastern Asia.

1 A wandering cockroach fails to notice a tailless whip scorpion half hidden in a gap under a rock.

2 Charging from cover, the killer snatches up the prey with its huge "claws." The insect tries to wriggle free, but the assassin tightens its grip. The whip scorpion bites into its body.

Did You Know?

● Some tailless whip scorpions are agile enough to snatch flying moths out of the air with their claws.

● Tailless whip scorpions have special brushes on their claws, which they use for grooming their bodies. And their mouthparts have rows of projections that can be rubbed against each other to produce grasshopperlike chirps.

● When two male tailless whip scorpions meet, they threaten each other with their clawlike pedipalps. If a female is around, the rivals get even more aggressive, grappling for an hour or more until one gives way. The winner of the battle is then free to court the female, vibrating his long front legs at her enticingly to persuade her to mate with him.

● Also known as whip spiders, tailless whip scorpions make useful houseguests, hiding in crevices and emerging at night to kill household pests such as cockroaches.

BARK SCORPION

Latin name: *Centruroides* species

TAIL

The bark scorpion's tail is longer and thinner than those of other scorpions. It's tipped with a hollow sting for injecting venom.

CLAWS

Slender crablike claws allow the scorpion to grasp its prey.

LEGS

Strong legs and sharp claws let the bark scorpion clamber up rocks and trees.

CHELICERAE

After subduing its prey, the bark scorpion dismembers the body with the spiky "teeth" of its moveable *chelicerae*.

A close encounter with this unusual climbing scorpion could have fatal consequences—and this American insect has a nasty habit of creeping into people's homes.

Bark scorpions are expert climbers. They often avoid the harsh heat of day by crawling under loose bark in low trees and shrubs. Concealed 3 feet or more above ground, they're well hidden both from predators and unwary humans—unless disturbed.

HOW BIG IS IT?

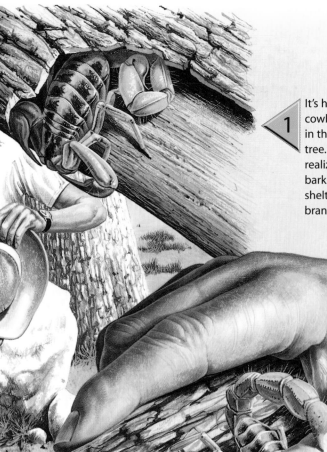

1 It's hot, and a cowboy stops to rest in the shade of a tree. He doesn't realize that a deadly bark scorpion is sheltering on a branch above.

2 He grips the branch to pull himself up and accidentally touches the scorpion. The insect strikes swiftly with its sting before scuttling off to a new hiding place.

BUG FACTS

LENGTH	2–4 in, depending on species
LIFESTYLE	Nocturnal predator
PREY	Insects and other invertebrates
WEAPONS	Stinger in tail armed with paralyzing venom

Bark scorpions prefer warm, dry habitats and are found from southern California across to Georgia and Florida, down through Arizona, New Mexico, and Texas to Nicaragua, Costa Rica, Panama, and Colombia. They also live on several islands in the Caribbean.

Did You Know?

● Some bark scorpions live close to the sea, foraging for food on the dry sand above the high–tide line.

● In the past, doctors often gave morphine–based painkillers to the victims of bark-scorpion stings, until they realized that these increased convulsive activity and the chances of death. Today, the most effective treatment is a combination of close support care and the intravenous injection of large doses of antivenom.

● The ancient Egyptians believed that young scorpions crawled from the corpses of crocodiles, and that women were immune to their stings.

● Folk remedies for a scorpion sting include making "tea" from the offending creature, eating it—either raw or cooked—or crushing its head and rubbing it into the wound.

● Most scorpions react strongly to light, and can die of dehydration if deprived of shade for too long.

GIANT MILLIPEDE

Latin name: Class Diplopoda

COLORS

Bright colors warn
predators that this
animal tastes bad.

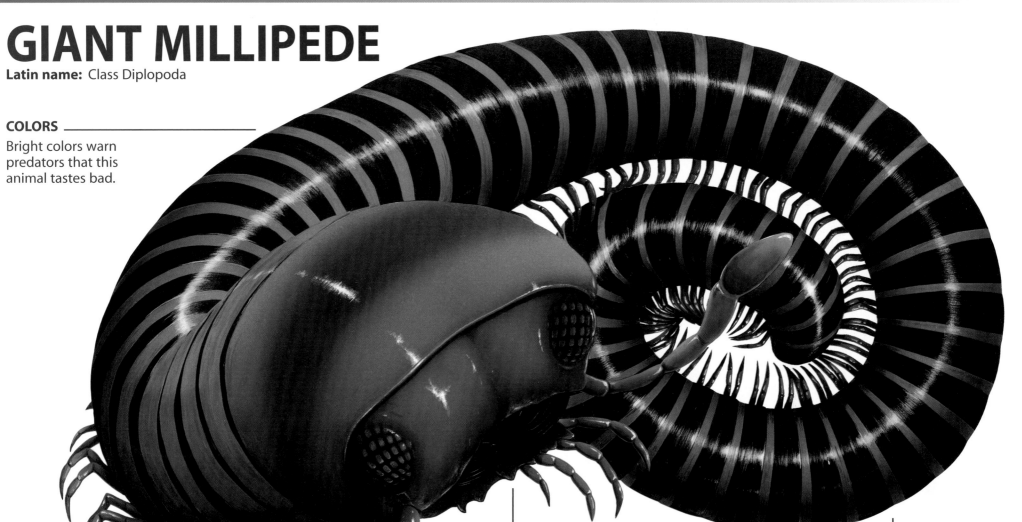

LEGS

There are two pairs of
legs for each body
segment. Centipedes
have only a single pair.

HEAD

There are two pairs of
mouthparts for biting and
grinding up food. Two
antennas provide sensory
information, as do tiny eyes.

CUTICLE

The tough cuticle
(body wall) is
reinforced with
calcium salts.

In cooler areas millipedes rarely grow very large, but tropical millipedes can grow up to 12 inches in length. Like their smaller cousins, these giant millipedes live in the soil, eating rotten plant matter and helping to aerate and nourish the ground. Having hundreds of legs is useful for burrowing in the soil, but a millipede can't run fast. So when predators threaten it fights back by releasing fluids that blister skin and blind eyes.

HOW BIG IS IT?

1 ▷ On the Indian Ocean island of Madagascar, a young tenrec is hunting. The hedgehoglike mammal usually picks on grubs its own size. This youngster is inexperienced and tries to tackle a giant millipede!

2 ▷ At first the millipede just coils, baring its armored sides. But as the tenrec persists, toxic fluids ooze from pores in the millipede's sides. Once these enter the tenrec's eyes, the mammal stumbles away, blinded.

BUG FACTS

LENGTH	Up to 12 in, depending on species
NUMBER OF BODY SEGMENTS	Up to 180, although most giants have fewer than 90
NUMBER OF LEGS	Usually 200 to 300, but some have very many more
DIET	Decaying organic matter on and in the soil
DEFENSES	Tough body shell; toxic or evil-smelling fluids leaked or sprayed from glands
LIFESPAN	10 years or more

Millipedes are found worldwide, but the real giants are mostly restricted to the tropics. They can be found in Central and South America, east to equatorial Africa (including Madagascar), and in southeastern Asia.

Did You Know?

● *Epibolus tanganyicense*, a giant millipede of East Africa, can spray its defensive fluids up to 16 inches away.

● Newly hatched millipedes have only four or five body segments, adding them as they age.

● The toxins of some millipedes are chemically similar to some of the drugs prescribed by doctors to help people relax. The millipede uses its chemicals to "relax" predators that try to bite it, like big spiders.

● Giant millipede fluids were used in a traditional Malay poison, along with "bile of toad and crow." The potion caused victims to cough up blood, then keel over and die.

EARWIG

Latin name: *Forficula auricularia*

BODY

Thin and flat, the earwig can slip into tiny spaces. Its flexible body lets it turn around easily to slip out again.

PINCERS

The strong tail pincers have sharp points. They open and close like nutcrackers.

WINGS

The thin, delicate hind wings are protected by a shell formed by the forewings.

ANTENNAS

These find food and warn of danger. They do this by tasting scents in the air and by detecting slight vibrations.

FEET

Each ends in a claw, giving excellent grip, even when the insect is upside down.

EYES

Compound eyes give good vision. At night the earwig finds its way around mainly by scent.

JAWS

Simple, biting jaws allow the earwig to deal with a wide variety of foods.

nstantly recognizable, with its slim brown body and distinctive tail "claw," the common earwig is a secretive little insect. It holes up in dark nooks and crannies by day, and hunts and scavenges by night. The earwig's real-life care of its young is just as extraordinary as its mythical enthusiasm for burrowing into people's ears. Fearless in the defense of her young, the female earwig challenges any creature that dares to approach her nest. Arching her tail over her back, she flourishes her forceps threateningly.

HOW BIG IS IT?

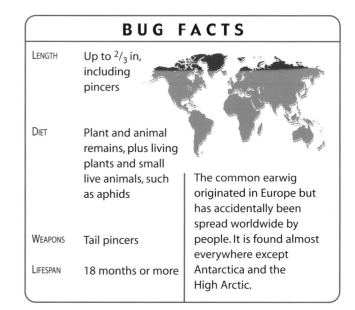

Actual Size

BUG FACTS

LENGTH	Up to $2/3$ in, including pincers	
DIET	Plant and animal remains, plus living plants and small live animals, such as aphids	The common earwig originated in Europe but has accidentally been spread worldwide by people. It is found almost everywhere except Antarctica and the High Arctic.
WEAPONS	Tail pincers	
LIFESPAN	18 months or more	

1

As her eggs develop in the nest, a mother earwig keeps them healthy by washing them and turning them to keep them at a constant temperature.

A male earwig appears on the scene, drawn by the smell of eggs. The mother instantly raises her armed tail high.

2

3 Spurred on by the powerful instinct to protect her eggs, the female charges and seizes the male with her strong pincers. He struggles briefly, but is powerless to resist the crushing force of her tail snippers.

Did You Know?

 ● Although the female earwig is a devoted mother, she can't recognize her own young once they leave the nest and later may eat them by mistake. On the other hand, the young may eat their mother in the nest if she dies from starvation while caring for them.

● Earwigs belong to the insect order *Dermaptera*, which means "skin-wing." This refers to the way their lacy wings resemble the tissuelike skin that peels off you when you are burned by the sun.

● By day in spring, summer, and fall, and throughout the whole of winter, hundreds of earwigs may gather in one cozy place to sleep.

● In Borneo, the earwig *Arixenia esau* lives in the fur of a small bat. At 1-inch long, it's a large parasite: On a human scale, it would be like having a lobster clinging to our body! The earwig itself carries bat fleas around—41 in one recorded case.

WOOD TERMITE

Latin name: Family Kalotermitidae

HEAD

Most soldier termites have long heads, covered by a hard shell for protection. But some species have short, flat heads that they use to block any holes in the tunnel walls.

ABDOMEN

The waistless abdomen is soft, and so pale that the stomach contents show through.

JAWS

Soldiers are equipped with powerful jaws for biting or wrestling with intruders.

ANTENNAS

Soldier termites find their way around using their antennas, which are sensitive to smell. The termites communicate by giving off special scents.

ood termites live in large colonies and perform a valuable role in nature, digesting and recycling dead and dying wood. The scurrying insects can chomp their way through billions of tons of dead wood every year. However, they are much less welcome if they happen to be living in a house. Once they start chewing up the timber, the damage may be irreparable. The only effective way to deal with an infestation of wood termites is to call in pest controllers.

HOW BIG IS IT?

Actual Size

1 A man walks eagerly to the door of his newly rented home. But there's a nasty surprise in store. Termites have been at work for many years, munching their way through the wood.

2 He steps onto the veranda with a heavy box under his arm. The tunnel-riddled wood gives way with a loud crack. He plunges through the floorboards, breaking an ankle in the process.

BUG FACTS

LENGTH	Immature nymph: up to $1/2$ in, soldier: up to $4/5$ in, queen up to $6/7$ in
HABITAT	Nests in dry tree trunks, branches, or exposed timbers
DIET	Dead and drying wood; also dead bodies of colony members, which provide a useful source of protein
BREEDING	Eggs hatch into male and female nymphs, which are capable of developing into reproductives or soldiers
LIFESPAN	About 1 year

Dry wood termites of the family *Kalotermitidae* abound in tropical and subtropical regions of the world. There are about 350 species in all, and they are particularly rife in coastal regions and on islands.

Did You Know?

● We often move wood termites from place to place in packing cases, furniture, and other wooden objects.

● In 1951, a great flood hit Kansas, submerging a termite-infested warehouse for seven days. But after workmen shoveled out the mud, the exterminators found the termites still chewing happily away.

● Wood termites prefer to keep under cover, and if they run out of food, they may build small tubes of earth or stalactitelike structures to access beams in nearby houses.

● Some species pass hexagonal-shaped fecal pellets, which they kick out of exit holes at the surface.

SILVERFISH

Latin name: *Lepisma sacharina*

LEGS

The silverfish has only short legs but it is a fast runner.

JAWS

The biting jaws are simple but effective. They, easily chomp through tough, fibrous foods.

PALPS

The antennas are too long to use at close quarters. The silverfish has two pairs of hairy, jointed palps, which it uses to explore its close surroundings.

TAIL

The tail is tipped by three long filaments called cerci. These are sensitive to touch.

BODY

There is no trace of wings, but there are often signs of extra legs.

ANTENNAS

Long antennas are the main sensory organs. They are sensitive to both touch and taste.

EYES

The silverfish's eyes are very small and are probably not very efficient.

Switch on a light as you enter a room and you may spot one of Earth's oldest, oddest creatures sharing your home. Silverfish belong to a primitive group of insects called the bristletails. These were among the first insects on Earth and have stayed more or less unchanged for almost 300 million years. Silvertails lead a secretive nightlife, foraging, feeding on unlikely materials, such as paper and glue, and practicing extraordinary limbo dances with their breeding partners.

HOW BIG IS IT?

x3

BUG FACTS

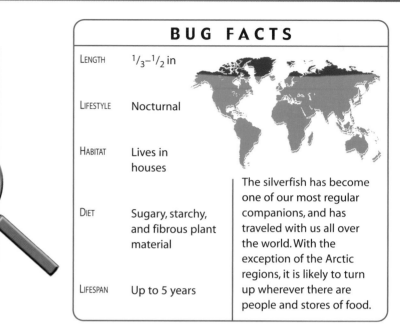

LENGTH	$1/3$–$1/2$ in
LIFESTYLE	Nocturnal
HABITAT	Lives in houses
DIET	Sugary, starchy, and fibrous plant material
LIFESPAN	Up to 5 years

The silverfish has become one of our most regular companions, and has traveled with us all over the world. With the exception of the Arctic regions, it is likely to turn up wherever there are people and stores of food.

1 When a male prepares to mate, he engages his partner in a lively dance. His antennas vibrate with excitement.

Soon the male spins a thread of silk. He attaches it between a raised surface and the ground. He carefully places a package of sperm underneath, then waits for the female to make her move.

2

3 The female performs a limbo dance under the thread with her tail raised. As her tail bristles strike the thread, she lowers her body to find the sperm capsule and gathers it up.

Did You Know?

● Some species of silverfish live in ant nests, and have even been observed trying to steal a quick snack as one ant passes food to another.

● Silverfish are difficult to catch because their tiny, silver scales simply come away in your fingers.

● Although silverfish may seem like pests, especially if they eat rare books and valuable pictures, they also clear up spilled food and other debris—so they can be useful insects to have around the house.

● Silverfish are also known as sugar-mites, because of their habit of nibbling on sweet groceries.

● Although silverfish have only one small pair of compound eyes, they react so quickly to the light, it seems probable that their whole body is sensitive to illumination.

● Bristletails are named after the fringes of hair on their tail filaments.

ANTLION
Latin name: *Myrmeleon formicarius* and others

LEGS

As the antlion digs a pit, it vibrates its forelegs to compact the sand and strengthen the walls. The back legs are modified for digging.

BRISTLES

Underneath, the body is covered with forward-pointing bristles. These prevent the larva from being pulled out of its burrow.

JAWS

The long, spiked, lower jaws are used to seize prey in a secure grip. The upper jaws form sharp tubes for injecting venom and sucking up body juices.

HEAD

The flattened head forms a miniature shovel for hurling sand.

EYES

Although the larva has large, eyes, it is very shortsighted. Sometimes, the antlion bombards objects with sand, thinking they are living prey.

Buried in sand, the antlion spends most of its life as a predatory larva, preparing for a short summer of adulthood when it will fly and mate. Energy for the brief breeding season comes from years of trapping and consuming prey. The antlion larva's funnel pit is a superb feat of engineering, particularly as the larva can only dig backward. Once it's built, the larva simply waits for other insects to drop in for dinner.

HOW BIG IS IT?

x2

BUG FACTS

LENGTH	Larva $1/4$–$1/3$ in; adult $1 4/5$ in
WINGSPAN OF ADULT	$2 1/2$ in
DIET	Larva: ants, spiders, and woodlice; adult: aphids, pollen, and nectar
PIT DIMENSIONS	1–2 in by 1–$2 3/4$ in
TIME SPENT DIGGING PIT	15 minutes
LIFESPAN	Larva: up to 3 years; adult: just a few weeks

Pit-building antlion species need to live in dry sand or dust. They are found mainly in tropical and subtropical regions of Asia, Australasia, and the Americas, although some live in central and northern Europe.

1 Buried in the bottom of its pit, the antlion larva waits for prey to stumble into its trap. A wandering ant peers curiously over the rim.

2 The antlion quickly scoops sand onto its head and flicks it straight at the ant. The ant loses its footing and tumbles down in a shower of sand.

3 When the ant reaches the bottom of the pit, the antlion grabs its victim. It pulls the ant into the sand and injects it with a paralyzing chemical.

Did You Know?

● The antlion larva feeds on fluids, and has no means of getting rid of waste. For several years the larva has to store waste products inside its body, so when it turns into an adult, one of the first things it does is excrete them.

● Three times in its larval life, the antlion leaves its pit to shed its skin as it grows. Each time, the larva stays hidden for up to ten days as its new skin hardens.

● The antlion larva can survive several months without food. When the temperature falls at the onset of cool weather, the larva usually stops feeding, lying dormant deep in its burrow until warmth returns.

HARVESTMAN

Latin name: Order Opiliones

BODY

A hard "shell" protects their back. The eyes are usually mounted on a stalk near the front.

SPIKE

Some harvestmen have sharp body spikes. These deter large predators from swallowing them.

LEGS

Many harvestmen have long, thin legs that can be up to 10 times their body length.

SECOND LEG

Some harvestmen walk around with their second pair of legs held high in the air. They use them like an extra-long pair of feelers.

LEG JOINT

In times of crisis, a harvestman may abandon its own leg to get away.

PEDIPALPS

A harvestman seizes its prey with its pedipalps. These come in different shapes and sizes. Some are short and spiky, others are longer and more leglike.

A harvestman looks and moves like a spider, but that's where the similarity ends. With just two eyes, an egg-laying tube, and the ability to eat solid food, these fast, eight-legged creatures are unique. There are 5,000 different species worldwide, some smaller than a grain of rice and others with a leg span as big as your hand. Tottering along on near-invisible legs, the harvestman barely seems able to support its plump body. But it's an efficient predator with an unusual hunting technique.

HOW BIG IS IT?

Actual Size

Creeping along on long, threadlike legs, a large harvestman is almost invisible against the leaf litter. Soon it senses movement nearby—a smaller relative on the prowl. The big harvestman isn't fussy about what it eats. It tiptoes forward until it towers above its unsuspecting prey.

1

Suddenly the harvestman drops onto its victim. The smaller animal claws desperately at the ground but the attacker holds fast. Moments later, the harvestman slices through its victim's outer shell and begins to shovel chunks of flesh into its mouth.

2

BUG FACTS

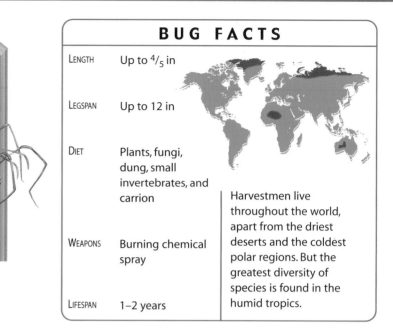

LENGTH	Up to ⁴/₅ in	
LEGSPAN	Up to 12 in	
DIET	Plants, fungi, dung, small invertebrates, and carrion	
WEAPONS	Burning chemical spray	
LIFESPAN	1–2 years	

Harvestmen live throughout the world, apart from the driest deserts and the coldest polar regions. But the greatest diversity of species is found in the humid tropics.

Did You Know?

● When some harvestmen are attacked, they gather a mixture of feces and other bodily secretions in their pedipalps and thrust it into the face of their unsuspecting assailant.

● If harvestmen don't drink plenty of fluids, they gradually become stiff and sluggish. In emergencies, they have even been known to drink ink.

● Although the female harvestman is usually the one to find a safe spot for her eggs, the male of one South American species not only builds a nest, but stays to guard both the eggs and the newly hatched young.

● Many harvestmen have such long pedipalps, they can lose all but one of their legs and still creep around.

● People sometimes refer to the harvestman by the common name of daddy longlegs, but as the term is also used to describe both a cellar spider and a type of stilt-legged fly, this can cause some confusion.

HUMAN LOUSE

Latin name: *Pediculus humanus & Phthirus pubis*

MOUTHPARTS

These act like a miniature syringe. When not in use, they are stored in a protective pouch.

CLAWS

Head and body lice have small, curved claws that curl around fine hairs and fabric fibers.

ANTENNAS

These stumpy feelers have chemical sensors so the louse can find its way around its host.

EYES

When its tiny eyes detect light, the louse's reaction is to run and hide.

LEGS

Head and body lice have six short, strong legs. It can hold onto a single hair or fiber using only one claw.

BODY

A flattened body allows the louse to slip between hairs easily. But when a louse feeds, its body fills with blood, swelling like a balloon.

Lice are the most common human parasites on the planet. Different types of lice are adapted to living on different areas of the body. One type, the body louse, can also carry a deadly disease.

Lice are well adapted for life in the hair jungle. By holding on tightly with their clawed feet, they can easily survive even the monsoon rain of a power shower. Every few hours, a louse slips its needlelike mouthparts into its host's skin and painlessly sucks their blood.

HOW BIG IS IT?

x7

1 The head louse has a slim body so it can move easily through the narrow spaces between head hairs. Its tiny claws can grip the finest strands of hair. The body louse uses its claws to cling onto the fine fibers of clothing.

2 The crab louse has huge, wide-apart claws for gripping thick, widely spaced body hairs, such as those found in armpits or beards.

3 When female head lice lay eggs, they glue them individually to strands of hair. The female body louse lays her eggs in the seams of her host's clothing, cementing them to fibers. Lice eggs hatch after about a week.

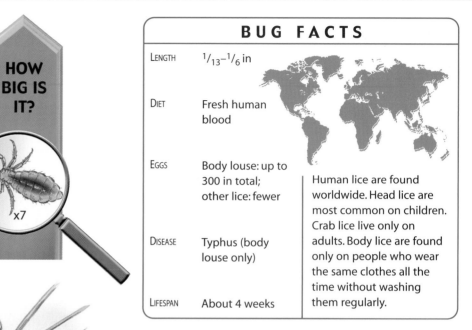

BUG FACTS

LENGTH	$1/13$–$1/6$ in
DIET	Fresh human blood
EGGS	Body louse: up to 300 in total; other lice: fewer
DISEASE	Typhus (body louse only)
LIFESPAN	About 4 weeks

Human lice are found worldwide. Head lice are most common on children. Crab lice live only on adults. Body lice are found only on people who wear the same clothes all the time without washing them regularly.

Did You Know?

● Lice and their eggs have been found mummified along with their hosts in ancient Egyptian tombs.

● Over 10,000 body lice were found in the shirt of one individual.

● The hard skin of a head louse can withstand a pressure of about 500,000 times the insect's own weight without cracking.

● For some reason, some people with head lice don't feel any itchiness after they have been bitten, so they don't scratch—and end up with hundreds of lice in their hair.

● The Aztec people—the main civilization in Mexico until the sixteenth century—ritually honored their rulers with gifts. In the case of the poor, these were small bags of lice painstakingly collected day after day.

● In parts of northern Siberia, women once courted men by throwing their body lice at them.

WOODLOUSE

Latin name: *Porcellio scaber*

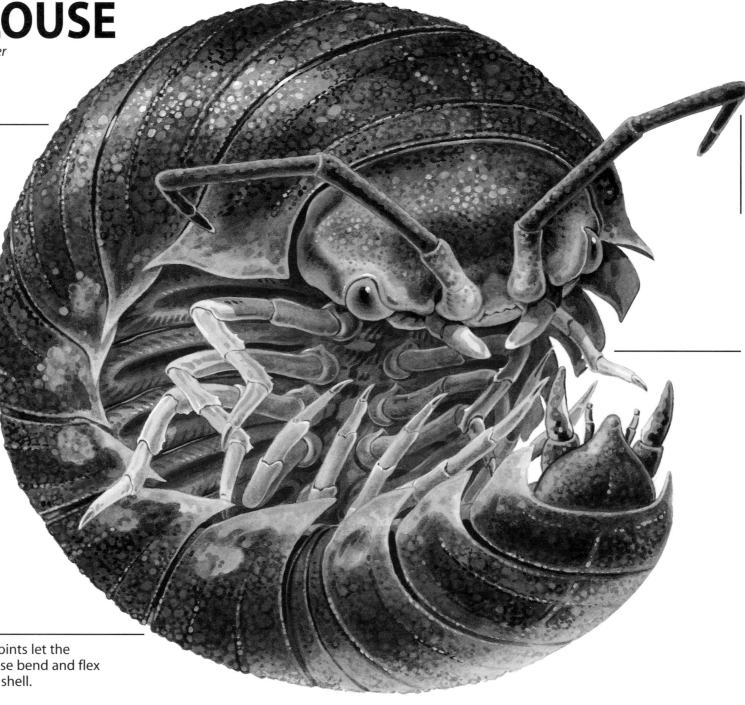

SKELETON

The shell lacks the waterproof waxy layer found on insects. This means the woodlouse dries out quickly when exposed to the air.

ARMOR

The jointed plates of the armor protect the soft belly.

JOINTS

Narrow joints let the woodlouse bend and flex the hard shell.

ANTENNAS

The main pair of antennas are long and jointed.

MOUTHPARTS

Modified legs on the head form the mouthparts.

The woodlouse is one of the few land-dwelling crustaceans and a close relative of crabs and lobsters. This shady beast likes to hide in cool, damp spots and comes out at night to feast on dead and dying plant matter. It excretes the nutrients from the plants back into the soil, making it one of nature's top recyclers.

Foul-tasting body fluids and a layer of tough armor protect this little crustacean from most predators. But it doesn't stand a chance against a foe like the woodlouse-eating spider, with its armor-piercing fangs.

HOW BIG IS IT?

Actual Size

BUG FACTS

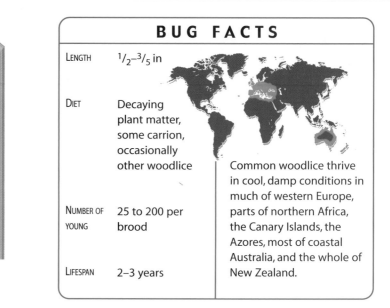

LENGTH	$1/2$–$3/5$ in
DIET	Decaying plant matter, some carrion, occasionally other woodlice
NUMBER OF YOUNG	25 to 200 per brood
LIFESPAN	2–3 years

Common woodlice thrive in cool, damp conditions in much of western Europe, parts of northern Africa, the Canary Islands, the Azores, most of coastal Australia, and the whole of New Zealand.

1 After a restful day spent in a dark, damp compost heap, three woodlice creep out at dusk to feed.

2 The peaceful meal is shattered by a woodlouse-eating spider. This sinister hunter has a pair of huge fangs for impaling prey. It can even give humans a nasty nip.

3 Each woodlouse tries a different means of escape. One curls up to protect its underparts. Another scuttles away into cover. But the third is out of luck. The spider flips it over and sinks its fangs into the victim's soft belly. It injects venom to liquefy the insides, which it then drinks up.

Did You Know?

● Young woodlice have only six body segments. The seventh segment with the seventh pair of legs appears only after the first molt.

● When Isaac Asimov, the famous scientist and writer, was young, he filled his mouth with woodlice to see if they tickled his tongue as they walked around. Apparently they did, but his mother was unimpressed.

● In Britain the woodlouse is known also as the grammar sow, tiggy-hog, sow-bug, and parson's pig.

● The pill bug is a relative of the woodlouse and looks quite similar. But while the woodlouse can only curl into a banana shape, the pill bug rolls itself fully into a ball.

● If it needs to, a woodlouse can survive by eating only paper and digesting the cellulose it contains.

● Instead of producing urine, the woodlouse excretes ammonia gas.

FALSE SCORPION

Latin name: Order Pseudoscorpiones

PEDIPALPS

The lobsterlike claws deliver venom through the hollow, spiked tips.

ABDOMEN

The blunt abdomen is covered with sensory hairs. If the hairs are touched, the animal spins and attacks.

MOUTHPARTS

These inject prey with digestive juices.

SENSORY HAIRS

With poor eyesight, the false scorpion depends on sensitive, hairlike organs to detect and identify prey and predators.

A false scorpion lacks the sting in the tail of a real scorpion, but it is still a fierce and efficient hunter. Powerful venom is delivered through its long pincers and it can kill surprisingly large prey. Many false scorpions migrate to new areas by hitching a ride. The carrier could be a fly, a large beetle, or a mammal such as a mole. Usually the host is unharmed, despite being seized in venomous claws. But false scorpions have been know to eat the host at the end of the trip.

HOW BIG IS IT?

x5

BUG FACTS

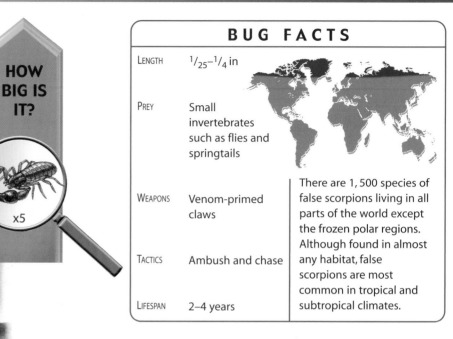

LENGTH	$^1/_{25}$–$^1/_4$ in
PREY	Small invertebrates such as flies and springtails
WEAPONS	Venom-primed claws
TACTICS	Ambush and chase
LIFESPAN	2–4 years

There are 1,500 species of false scorpions living in all parts of the world except the frozen polar regions. Although found in almost any habitat, false scorpions are most common in tropical and subtropical climates.

1

A false scorpion seizes a springtail in its sharp-tipped claws. A deadly chemical quickly floods into the wounds, killing the victim.

2 The false scorpion uses its mouthparts to inject the corpse with juices that dissolve its insides. It then sucks up the resulting mush.

Did You Know?

● Bulging with a meal of juices sucked from a plump victim, a false scorpion may go for weeks or even months before feeding again.

● Most false scorpions have two or four rudimentary little eyes, but those species that spend their entire lives hunting in the total darkness of caves don't have any eyes at all.

● The false scorpion's greatest claim to fame is that it is the only animal that can run backward faster than it can run forward.

● In a scientific experiment, a false scorpion regained dry land after "falling" into water by climbing "hand-over-hand" up a human hair, like a sailor climbing up a rope, using only its lobsterlike claws.

● Scorpions, spiders, and false scorpions are truly ancient critters. The earliest known false scorpions lived about 380 million years ago, during the Devonian period.

GIANT CENTIPEDE
Latin name: *Scolopendra* species

TAIL LEGS

The legs at the end of the tail are used for fighting or holding prey.

POISON CLAWS

A large pair of claws deliver the death blow. Muscles squeeze venom out of a hole at the tip.

BODY SEGMENTS

Tough plates of skin cover the body, protecting it from attack. Each section can move separately, letting the centipede move freely.

The giant centipede glides at breakneck speed through rotting leaf litter in pursuit of prey. Its venomous claws are always ready for attack. Like the fangs of many snakes, these sharp-pointed pincers are capable of injecting a killer mix of toxins.

All centipedes are predators, hunting down live prey, but the giant centipede can tackle birds, rats, mice, and even snakes.

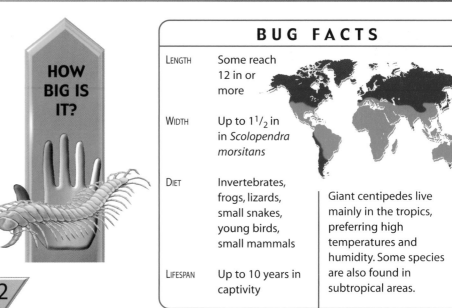

HOW BIG IS IT?

BUG FACTS

LENGTH	Some reach 12 in or more
WIDTH	Up to 1½ in in *Scolopendra morsitans*
DIET	Invertebrates, frogs, lizards, small snakes, young birds, small mammals
LIFESPAN	Up to 10 years in captivity

Giant centipedes live mainly in the tropics, preferring high temperatures and humidity. Some species are also found in subtropical areas.

1

A giant centipede detects prey with its antennas, and moves in for the kill. Its stout claws are full of venom.

The chosen victim is a wren finch. The centipede's claws pinch into the bird's flesh. Venom streams into the puncture wounds. Centipedes vary the amount of venom injected according to the prey. Large tropical species can kill a mouse or small bird almost instantly.

2

Did You Know?

● A 4-inch-long centipede in the United States was once observed killing and carrying off a 10-inch-long snake.

● Giant centipedes can rear up to snatch bees and wasps out of the air with their claws.

● Centipedes were given their name in the belief that they had 100 legs (*centi* comes from the Latin for "hundred" and *pede* from the word for "feet"). In fact, some species have as few as 30 legs and others as many as 362. Giant centipedes have 21 to 23 pairs of legs.

● Centipedes are among the most ancient of all land-dwelling creatures. Scientists have found fossilized centipede bodies that are 414 million years old, and centipede footprints that date back an incredible 450 million years.

● Big nerve fibers carry messages at lightning speed, so the centipede can react almost instantaneously.

The giant centipede curls around the dead bird to start feeding on its plump body. The predator cuts the body into bite-sized fragments.

3

WIND SPIDER

Latin name: *Solifugae* species

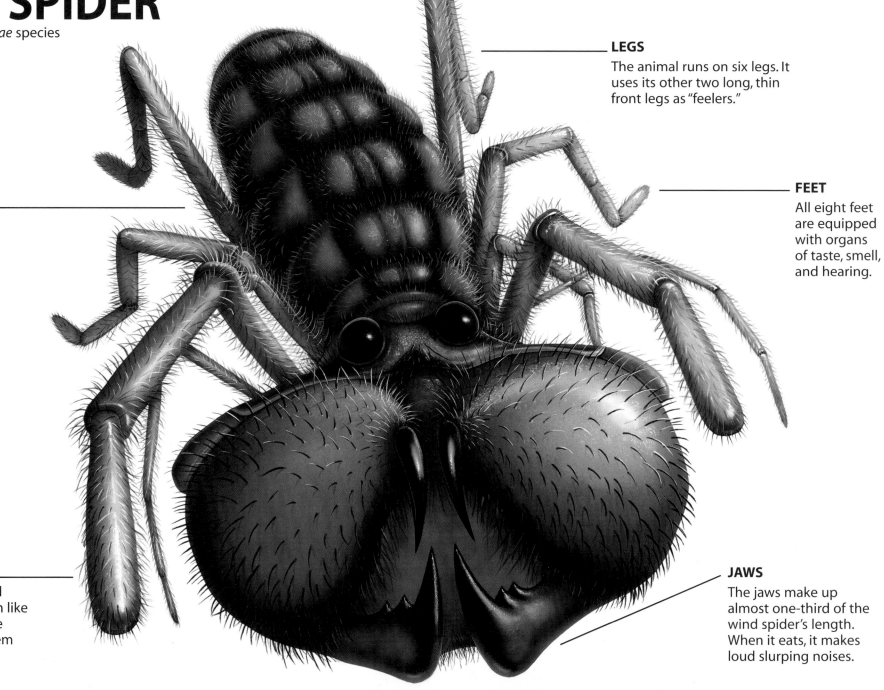

LEGS
The animal runs on six legs. It uses its other two long, thin front legs as "feelers."

FEET
All eight feet are equipped with organs of taste, smell, and hearing.

SKIN
A hard, waxy cuticle, or "skin," covers the body. In some species, this gives off small amounts of ultraviolet radiation, so at night a wind spider may glow purple under UV light.

PEDIPALPS
Mobile organs called pedipalps look much like a pair of legs. But the wind spider uses them like a pair of hands.

JAWS
The jaws make up almost one-third of the wind spider's length. When it eats, it makes loud slurping noises.

A wind spider is an eight-legged shredding machine. These vicious killers have the largest jaws of any living creature, relative to body size. They can also run like the wind, so few small animals can escape the pulverizing grip of their powerful killing apparatus.

Covered with vibration-sensitive hairs, there is nothing cuddly about these hyperactive hunters. Wind spiders are constantly in search of prey to mince and gorge to restore their energy levels.

1 A wind spider dashes over the desert sand. Hairs bristling on its body tell it information about its surroundings. It detects the vibrations created by a little lizard. Rushing over, it seizes the startled gecko in its long pedipalps.

HOW BIG IS IT?

Actual Size

BUG FACTS

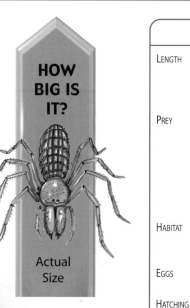

LENGTH	1–3 in, depending on species
PREY	Insects, scorpions, spiders, and other wind spiders; large species prey on young birds, lizards, and rodents; carrion
HABITAT	Mountains, forests, deserts, plains, fields, and gardens
EGGS	20–200
HATCHING PERIOD	About 4 weeks, depending on environmental conditions
LIFESPAN	Up to 1 year

Wind spiders like warm climates. They are found in southern Canada, Central America, parts of South America, southern Spain, Africa, southern Asia from Saudi Arabia to India, Southeast Asia, and Sulawesi.

2 The wind spider flips the struggling lizard onto its back. It starts to eat it alive. The munching jaws soon liquidizes the lizard's flesh. The wind spider sucks up the gooey mass.

Did You Know?

● Wind spiders have voracious appetites and are sometimes released into crops to eat swarms of harmful grubs and beetles as an eco-friendly alternative to using pesticides.

● One captive wind spider, just over 1 inch long, was seen to devour more than 100 fruit flies in a single day.

● Wind spiders have highly mobile pedipalps, and some species can cup them like a pair of hands to carry water to their mouth. Each pedipalp has an adhesive organ at the tip, so the spider can even climb up glass.

● The earliest known wind spider lived more than 65 million years ago in Brazil, South America.

GLOSSARY

ABDOMEN
The hind part of the body of an insect.

ANTENNA
One of two long, slender organs on the head of an insect. Bugs and insects use these antennas to find their way around, search for food, and sometimes to communicate.

ARTHROPOD
An animal with jointed legs, an external skeleton, and a body divided into segments. Insects, spiders, and crustaceans are all types of arthropod.

CAMOUFLAGE
Many species of bug or insect hide from predators using some type of disguise or coloring that blends in with their surroundings. This is called camouflage. Stick insects disguise themselves as sticks and twigs, for example. Butterfly bugs have long, waxy fibers to camouflage themselves against moss or lichen growing on a branch.

CARNIVORE
A meat-eating creature. Bugs that feed on the flesh of insects and other types of animal are called carnivorous. Some types of insect are only carnivorous when they are young. Adult wasps, for example, drink the sugary nectar from flowers, but they feed their young larvae on meat.

CATERPILLAR
The long, wormlike larva of a butterfly or moth before it changes into an adult. Caterpillars are often brightly colored. They usually feed on leaves, fruit, or vegetables and can be very destructive.

COLONY
A population of insects living together and interacting with one another. Many types of bees, wasps, or ants live together in highly organized colonies. Each individual insect has its own particular job to do to help the whole colony prosper.

COMPOUND EYE
Many bugs and insects have compound eyes. This means that each eye is made up of lots and lots of tiny lenses. A fly's eye, for example, has around 4,000 lenses. Each lens forms a small picture of the world in front of it so that the bug sees the world in lots of tiny pictures. This doesn't give very clear vision, but it is good for spotting movement.

CRUSTACEAN
An animal with eight or more legs, two pairs of antennas, and a hard shell, or exoskeleton. Most crustaceans, such as crabs and lobsters, live in the water. A few, such as the woodlouse, live on land.

DIGESTION
To digest food means to change it into simpler and smaller forms so it can be taken in and used by the body to produce energy. Some bugs digest their food by covering it in juices to dissolve it and then sucking up the resulting liquid mush.

EXOSKELETON
The hard shell or outer covering of an insect. Insects have soft inner bodies without an internal skeleton. They need the hard exoskeleton on the outside of their body to keep their body shape. It often also provides protection against predators.

GERM
A tiny living organism, too small to see with the naked eye, especially one that causes disease. Some bugs, such as cockroaches or Chagas bugs, carry germs living on or inside their bodies. They may then spread these germs to humans if they come into contact with our food or our bodies.

GRUB
A soft, thick, wormlike young insect, before it turns into an adult.

HABITAT
A bug's habitat is the area in which it normally lives and grows. Different bugs are suited to different types of habitat. The woodlouse, for example, prefers cool, damp, dark habitats where it can stay moist and remain hidden from predators.

INFESTATION
A large number of harmful or irritating insects or other pests is called an infestation. For example, an infestation of scabies mites on the body would cause terrible itching. An infestation of Colorado beetles in a potato field might destroy the farmer's crop.

LARVA
The wingless and often wormlike form of many newly hatched insects. Many species of bugs go through this stage before changing into adults.

NYMPH
A young insect that has not yet grown into an adult, especially one that is smaller than the adult but looks recognizably similar.

ORGANISM
Any living plant or creature.

PARASITE
A bug or other creature that lives off another plant or animal, for example, by sucking blood or eating skin cells. The plant or animal that the parasite lives off is called the host. The parasite benefits but the host does not— indeed the parasite is often harmful or irritating to the host.

PEST
Any troublesome or destructive insect, animal, or plant. The Colorado beetle is a pest because it attacks and destroys potato crops. The scabies mite is a pest because it can cause severe itching.

PINCERS
Claspers that can be used for gripping onto prey, grasping food, or for defense. Some male bugs use their pincers to hold onto females during mating.

PREDATOR
An animal that hunts and kills other animals.

SCAVENGER
Some insects find and eat the remains of animals or plants that are already dead. Scavengers play a very important role in breaking down and recycling waste material.

THORAX
The bodies of all true insects are divided into three parts. The thorax is the middle body part, between the head and the abdomen.

TROPICAL
A tropical region of the world is one that lies close to Earth's equator, where the temperature is warm all year round. Bugs and insects are found all over the world, but many types of bug, including some of the biggest bugs, prefer hot, tropical regions.

VENOM
A poisonous fluid that is injected into a victim, usually by biting or stinging. Some bugs used their venom to kill or paralyze their prey, others use it only for self-defense.

INDEX

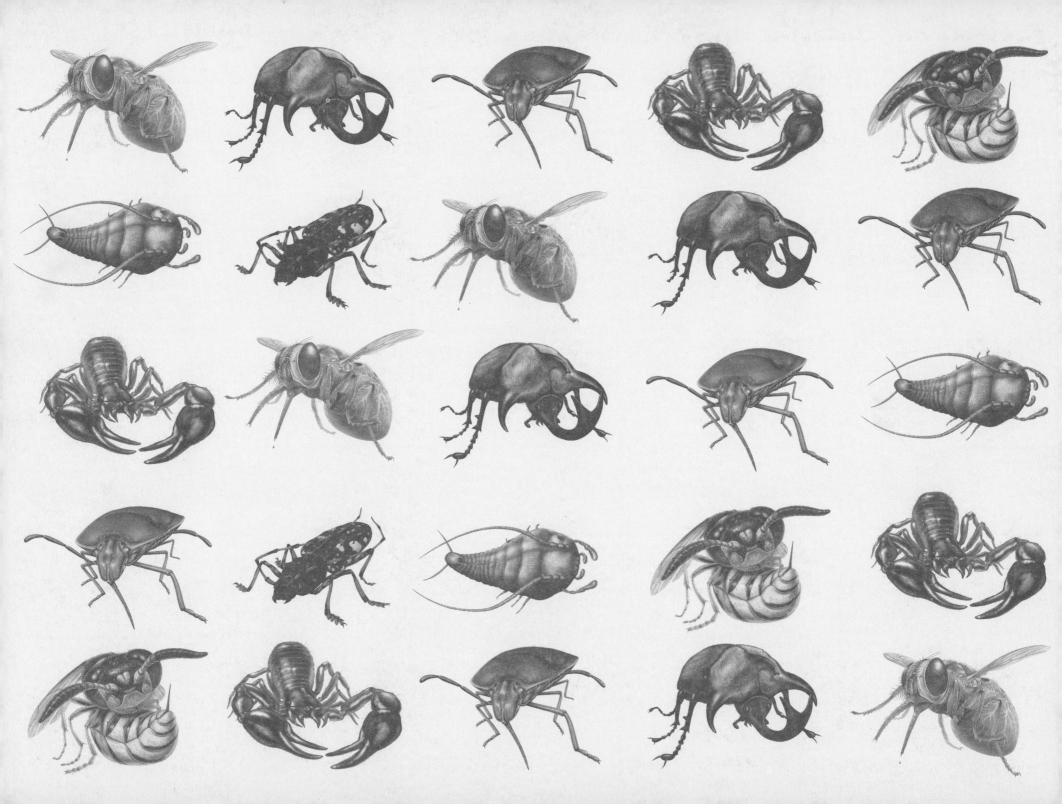